The MASTERS Of Success

12-3-08

Martin,

Dream Big!

INSIGHT PUBLISHING
SEVIERVILLE, TENNESSEE

© 2005 by Insight Publishing Company.

Published by Insight Publishing Company
P.O. Box 4189
Sevierville, Tennessee 37864

10 9 8 7 6 5 4 3 2

Printed in The United States

ISBN: 1-60013-010-0

Table Of Contents

A Message From The Publisher

Time is a precious commodity in the fast-paced world in which we live today. The amount of information available to us is so overwhelming there's just no keeping up with it all. Reading or word-of-mouth used to be the only way to disseminate information but today we have the Internet, radio, and television giving us instant access to all kinds of information including local and world events as they happen.

With time so valuable, sorting through the vast amount of information out there can be a daunting task. *Masters of Success* has been carefully put together to help you quickly learn tips and the inside information you need to live a full and successful life. This book contains some of the most interesting conversations I have ever had with several of the most successful people I have ever met.

The comparatively small amount of time you spend with this book will reward you with more information about success than you can find just about anywhere else. It is my pleasure to invite you to sit back, relax, and get ready to be inspired!

Interviews conducted by:
David E. Wright
President, International Speakers Network

Chapter One

MICHAEL BRAXTON

THE INTERVIEW

David E. Wright (Wright)

Today we're talking with Michael Braxton. Michael has been called "The Transformer" because he guides untrained sales managers through the basics and transforms them into powerful leaders of their sales teams. His company, Sales Manager 101, lives by the motto, "Isn't the key task of a sales manager to motivate, support, and extract results from the sales team; is there any more important position in the entire company?" Author and sales force management coach, Michael Braxton has been working with the sales teams of great companies like Kodak, Sinclair Oil Corporation, Teleflora, and FTD since 1986. Creator of the newest technique in sales force management, the SPA-Sales Performance Agreement, Michael has begun to revolutionize sales team management. "Sales reps are confused," Michael sometimes quips, "sales superstars are more likely to perform at a higher level when they know precisely what is expected of them." These SPA documents are a perfect tool for gaining agreement between management and the sales team as to exactly what is expected. Michael Braxton is the author of *Sales Manager 101: Learning System and Desktop Manual,* as well as other sales force management tools available on his Web site, www.salesmanager101.com.

Mr. Braxton, welcome to *Masters of Success*.

Michael Braxton (Braxton)
Thank you, I'm thrilled to be involved in this project.

Wright
I see from your bio you've been in sales for nineteen years. Would you tell our readers a little bit about yourself and how you ended up as President of Sales Manager 101?

Braxton
Truth is, I've been in sales all my life. In fact, I was the Boy Scout Christmas tree lot sales champ back when I was fourteen years old. Professionally, however, I've been working with sales organizations since 1986 and launched my own company to help create better sales managers.

Wright
When I Google "sales manager expert" your name comes up. What makes you an expert?

Braxton
Experience certainly plays a role, but what makes me an "expert"? I think it's more related to the research I conduct for the association called Professional Sales Force Managers International (www.psfmi.org). As the Chair, I read everything possible regarding the field of sales force management and consult with innovative, successful sales managers every day. I take theoretical information and superimpose these theories into *real-life* client situations. I evaluate new trends in sales management and often make recommendations to corporations and sales managers.

Wright
Michael, we're starting to hear you referred to as the "Sales Manager 101 Guru," is that a program you've developed? And if so, what inspired you?

Braxton
There are many untrained sales managers in America; they're sort-of winging it and making things up as they go along. I've worked

for a few of these unskilled managers myself. Many sales managers were promoted from rep to sales management and can harbor a skewed perspective. Without the training necessary to lead a sales force, they often get caught in their own "blind spots." That's to say their experience as a sales person gets them into trouble as sales manager. They *over-value* the wrong things and *under-value* the right things. Because there is such a gap between what sales managers know and what they *need* to know, I created Sales Manager 101.

Wright

So let me see if I get this. Promoting your number one sales guy to sales manager is not necessarily a great idea? And are you saying that great sales people are born and great sales managers are made?

Braxton

Yes, I am. Promoting your top-performing salesperson to manager is often a terrible idea. He or she got to be number one by harnessing personal skills opposite of those necessary to become a successful sales manager. Generally, sales superstars are loners—egocentric folks who make their own rules—not what you need to manage a sales team. In fact, when you promote such a superstar to management you deal yourself a double-whammy; you lose your number one salesperson and promote a bad choice to manager. Basically it's just not a good idea.

Wright

I thought sales people were driven by the mighty dollar or commission, isn't that true?

Braxton

There is no question that commission motivates sales people. But the fact that sales superstars are motivated by an internal need to persuade is undeniable. Great sales managers, on the other hand, can be taught the skills necessary for success; it's much more of a science that an art.

Wright

Obviously we can't give away all your secrets but what are the main techniques your Sales Manager 101 system addresses?

Braxton

The key is leadership. A strong respected leader is absolutely critical to creating a successful sales team. I'm an advocate for setting precise articulate goals and boundaries for the team members you manage. In fact, I've begun to work with documents called "Sales Performance Agreements" or SPAs. Think of these documents as contracts between sales people and management. They explicitly spell out expectations and gain agreement between the two parties. One fatal error sales managers make is not setting specific goals. This agreement virtually eliminates that problem.

Wright

Wow! "Fatal error" sounds scary. Give us a hint; would you tell me one more fatal error an untrained sales manager might make?

Braxton

Another fatal error of sales team leaders is wasting sales meetings. Sales meetings can be an incredibly valuable and motivational tool, yet most sales managers simply "get them over with." If you follow a few simple rules you'll achieve terrific results. For instance:

- Never be late. If you set an example of showing up a little tardy, even with a great excuse, the account execs will feel entitled to do the same thing and your control of the start time will begin to slip away.
- Bring treats.
- Always be positive.
- Never allow one bad apple to hijack the meeting with his or her own personal issues.
- Bring in customers from the real world to explain how they choose certain vendors. This could be incredibly useful to the team.

Wright

You seem like a practical, back-to-basics kind of consultant. That's different than most management consultants, isn't it?

Braxton

I focus on expanding the talent already in my client's team. My goal is to develop your thinking not sell mine.

Wright

Sounds as if you've found your calling and are following your passion. Are you happy with your life as a sales management coach and keynote speaker?

Braxton

Everything in my life has led me to this point. From selling Christmas trees as a Boy Scout to publishing the Sales Manager 101 learning system. I know that I'm doing exactly what I was meant to do—develop sales teams. I'm thrilled to be working in the field for which I have a passion.

Wright

In your twenty years experience, have you found that there are people who fit into profiles that make them better salespeople and those who do not?

Braxton

I think there are, David. Sales superstars have an internal need to persuade. This theory is supported by many studies and published in *Harvard Business Review* and *Selling Power Magazine*. You'll find that sales people with internal, intrinsic motivation that drives them are generally more successful than anyone else.

Wright

So, if I'm looking for a sales manager, should I go after people who are management-oriented rather than sales-oriented?

Braxton

I would look for someone who has some sales experience but is more of an *administrative* superstar. Successful sales managers are much more like secretaries and cheerleaders than sales superstars. It all comes down to leadership.

Wright

Your reputation precedes you. You've obviously been successful; so let me ask, what's next for Michael Braxton? Got any plans on the horizon?

Braxton

Well, my number one priority—making sales managers more effective—is keeping me busy but I am launching a new product next month specifically designed to help local sales managers in the media, television, and advertising field. I'm very excited about this new project.

You can check out the Web site www.LocalSalesManager.TV for more information.

Wright

Well, what a great conversation! I've learned a lot here today. I'm going to think about some of those hiring practices when I start looking for sales managers.

Braxton

Good luck, I'll be happy to help you even further if you'd like to give me a call.

Wright

Today we've been talking with Michael Braxton. He guides sales managers through the basics and transforms them into sales team leaders. Interestingly, he is the creator of the newest technique in sales force management, the SPA—Sales Performance Agreement. He's the author of *Sales Manager 101: Learning System and Desktop Manual,* as well as other sales force management tools available at www.salesmanager101.com.

Michael, thank you so much for being with us today on *Masters of Success.*

Braxton

It was a pleasure to be here, David.

About The Author

Isn't the key task of a sales manager to motivate, support, and extract results from the sales team… is there any more important position in the entire company? Do *you* have what it takes to lead a powerful sales team?

Log on to www.salesmanager101.com or www.localsalesmanager.tv to discover how to transform your sales force into the greatest sales team on earth.

Michael Braxton

Sales Manager 101 – Local Sales Manager (TV)

123 NW 12th Avenue, Suite #1231

Portland, OR 97209

Phone: 503.227.5239

Fax: 801.606.7344

Email: info@michaelbraxton.com

www.SalesManager101.com

www.LocalSalesManager.tv

Chapter Two

KEN BLANCHARD

David E. Wright (Wright)

Few people have created a positive impact on the day-to-day management of people and companies more than Dr. Kenneth Blanchard who is known around the world simply as Ken, a prominent, gregarious, sought after author, speaker, and business consultant. Ken is universally characterized by friends, colleagues, and clients as one of the most insightful, powerful, and compassionate men in the business today.

Ken's impact as a writer is far-reaching. His phenomenal best-selling book, *One Minute Manager*, co-authored with Spencer Johnson, has sold more than nine million copies worldwide and has been translated into more than twenty-five languages. Ken is Chairman and "Chief Spiritual Officer" of the Ken Blanchard Companies. The organization's focus is to energize organizations around the world with customized training in bottom line business strategies that are based on the simple yet powerful principles inspired by Ken's best-selling books.

Dr. Blanchard, welcome to *Masters of Success*!

Dr. Ken Blanchard (Blanchard)
Well, it's nice to talk to you, David. It's good to be here.

Wright
I must tell you that preparing for your interview took quite a bit more time than usual. The scope of your life's work and your business, the Ken Blanchard Companies, would make for a dozen fascinating interviews. Before we dive into the specifics of some of your projects and strategies, will you give our readers a brief synopsis of your life, how you came to be the Ken Blanchard we all know and respect?

Blanchard
Well, I'll tell you, David, I think life is what happens when you are planning on doing something else. I forget whose line that was; but I never intended to do what I have been doing. In fact, all my professors in college told me I couldn't write. I wanted to do college work, which I did. They told me, "You had better be an administrator." So I decided I was going to be a Dean of Men, a Dean of Students. I got provisionally accepted into my master's degree program, and then provisionally accepted at Cornell, because I never could take any of those standardized tests.

I took the College Boards four times and finally got 502 in English. My mind doesn't work. I ended up in a higher university in Athens, Ohio, in 1966 as Administrative Assistant to the Dean of the Business School. When I got there, he said, "Ken, I want you to teach a course. I want all my deans to teach." I had never thought about teaching because they said I couldn't write, and you had to publish.

He put me in the manager's department. I've taken enough bad courses in my day; I wasn't going to teach one. So I really prepared and had a wonderful time with the students. I was chosen as one of the top ten teachers on the campus coming out of the chute. I just had a marvelous time. A colleague by the name of Paul Hershey was chairman of the management department, and he wasn't real friendly to me initially because the Dean had led me into his department. But I heard he was a great teacher. He taught organizational behavior and leadership, so I asked him if I could sit in on his course next semester.

"Nobody audits my courses," he replied. "If you want to take it for credit, you're welcome." I couldn't believe it. I had a doctorate degree and he wanted me to take his course for credit. So I signed up. The registrar didn't know what to do with me because I already had a doctorate, but I wrote the papers and took the course, and it was great.

In June 1967, Hershey came into my office and said, "Ken, I've been teaching in this field for ten years. I think I'm better than anybody, but I can't write. I'm a nervous wreck, and I'd love to write a textbook with somebody. Would you write one with me?"

I said, "We ought to be a great team. You can't write and I'm not supposed to, so let's do it!" So thus began this great career of writing and teaching. We wrote a textbook called, *Management of Organizational Behavior Utilizing Human Resources*. It just came out with its eighth edition last year and it has sold more than any other textbook in its field throughout the years. It's been more than thirty-five years since that book came out.

I quit my administrative job, became a professor, and I worked my way up through the ranks. I took a sabbatical leave and went to California for one year twenty-five years ago. I met Spencer Johnson at a cocktail party. Spencer wrote children's books; he has a wonderful series called, *Value Tales for Kids: The Value of Courage: The Story of Jackie Robinson and The Value of Believing In Yourself: The Story Louis Pasteur*. My wife, Margie, met him first and told me, "You guys ought to write a book together—a children's book for managers, because they won't read anything else." That was my introduction to Spencer. So, our book, the *One Minute Manager* was really a kid's book for big people. That is a long way from saying my career was well planned.

Wright

Ken, what and/or who were your early influences in the areas of business, leadership, and success. In other words, who shaped you in your early years?

Blanchard

My father had a great impact on me. He was retired as an Admiral in the Navy and had a wonderful philosophy. I remember when I was elected to president of the seventh grade and I came home all pumped up. My father said, "Son, it's great that you're the president of the seventh grade, but now that you have that leadership position, don't ever use it." He said, "Great leaders are followed because people respect them and like them, not because they have power." That was a wonderful lesson for me early on. He was just a great model for me. I got a lot from him.

Then I had this wonderful opportunity in the mid 1980s to write a book with Norman Vincent Peale, author of, *The Power of Positive Thinking*. I met him when he was eighty-six years old. We were asked to write a book on ethics together and we wrote, *The Power of Ethical Management: Integrity Pays, You Don't Have to Cheat to Win*. It didn't matter what we were writing together, I learned so much from him; he just added to what I learned from my mother. When I was born my mother said, "I laughed before I cried, I danced before I walked, and I smiled before I frowned." So that, on top of Norman Vincent Peale, really made me I focus on what I could do to train leaders. I asked questions like: How do you make them positive? How do you make them realize that it's not about them—it's about those they are serving? It's not about their position—it's about what they can do to help other people win. So, I'd say my mother and father, and then Norman Vincent Peale had a tremendous impact on me.

Wright

I can imagine. I read a summery of your undergraduate and graduate degrees. I assumed you studied business administration, marketing management, and related courses. Instead, at Cornell you studied government and philosophy. You received your master's in sociology and counseling from Colgate and your Ph.D. from Cornell in educational administration and leadership. Why did you choose this course of study? How has it affected your writing and consulting?

Blanchard

Well, again, it wasn't really well planned out. I originally went to Colgate to get a master's degree in education, because I was going to be a Dean of Students over men. I had been a government major, and I was a government major because it was the best department in Cornell in the Liberal Arts School. It was exciting. We would study what the people were doing at the league governments.

The Philosophy Department was also great. I just loved the philosophical arguments. I wasn't a great student in terms of grades, but I'm a total learner. I would sit there and listen and I would really soak it in. When I went over to Colgate and got involved in the education courses, they were awful—they were boring. By the second week, I was sitting at the bar at the Colgate Inn saying, "I can't believe I've been here two years for this."

This is just the way the Lord works: sitting next to me in the bar was a young sociology professor who had just got his Ph.D. at Illinois, and his wife was back packing up. He was staying at the Inn and I was moaning and groaning about what I was doing. He said to me, "Why don't you come and major with me in sociology? It's really exciting."

"I can do that?" I asked.

He said, "Yes."

I knew they would probably let me do whatever I wanted the first week. Suddenly, I switched out of education and went with Warren Ramshaw. He had a tremendous impact on me. He retired a few years ago as the leading professor at Colgate in the Arts and Sciences, and he got me interested in leadership and organizations. That's why I got a master's in sociology.

Then the reason I went into educational administration and leadership was because it was a doctoral program I could get into. The reason for that was I knew the guy heading up the program, Don McCarty. He said, "The greatest thing about Cornell is that you will be in a School of Education. It's not very big, so you don't have to take many education courses, and you can take stuff all over the place." Don McCarty ended up going on to be the Dean of the School of Education, Wisconsin. He had an impact on my life, but I was always searching around.

My mission statement is, "To be a loving teacher and example of simple truths that help myself and others to awaken to the presence of God in our lives." The reason I mention God is, I believe the biggest addiction in the world is the human ego; I'm really into simple truth, however. I used to tell people I was trying to get the B.S. out of the behavioral sciences.

Wright

I can't help but think when you mentioned your father, that he just bottomed-lined it for you about leadership.

Blanchard

Yes.

Wright

Years ago when I went to a conference in Texas, a man named Paul Myers said, "David, if you think you're a leader and you look around, and no one is following you, you're just out for a walk."

Blanchard

Well, you'd get a kick out of this: I'm just reaching over to pick up a picture of Paul Myers on my desk; he's a good friend. We co-founded the Center for Faith Walk Leadership here where we're trying to challenge and equip people to lead like Jesus. It's non-profit, and I tell people I'm not an evangelist because we've got enough trouble with the Christians we have—we don't need any more new ones. But, there is a picture of Paul on top of a mountain, and then another picture below of him under the sea with stingrays. It says, "Attitude is everything. Whether you're on the top of the mountain or the bottom of the sea, true happiness is achieved by accepting God's promises, and by having a biblically positive frame of mind. Your attitude is everything." Isn't that something?

Wright

He's a fine, fine man. He helped me tremendously.

In keeping with the theme of our book, *The Masters of Success,* I wanted to get a sense from you about your own success journey. Many people know you best from the *One Minute Manager* books you coauthored with Spencer Johnson. Would you consider these books as a high water mark for you, or have you defined success for yourself in different terms?

Blanchard

Well, you know the *One Minute Manager* was an absurdly successful book. It achieved success so quickly I found I couldn't take credit for it. So that was when I really got on my own spiritual journey and started to try to find out what the real meaning of life and success was. It's been a wonderful journey for me because I think, David, the problem with most people is they think their self-worth is a function of their performance plus the opinion of others. The minute you define your self-worth like that, every day your self-worth is up for grabs because your performance is going to fluctuate on a day-to-day basis. People are fickle—their opinions are going to go up and down. So, you need to ground your self-worth in the unconditional love God has ready for us.

That concept grew out of the unbelievable success of the *One Minute Manager.* When I started to realize where all that came from, that's how I got involved in the ministry I mentioned. Paul Myers is a part of it. As I started to read the Bible, I realized that everything I've ever written about, or taught, Jesus did. You know, He did it with the twelve incompetent guys He hired. The only guy with much education was Judas, who was His only turnover problem.

Wright

Right.

Blanchard

So it was a really interesting thing. What I see in people is not only do they think their self-worth is a function of their performance plus the opinion of others, but do they measure their success on the amount of accumulation of wealth, on recognition, power, and status? I think those are nice success items—there's nothing wrong with those, as long as you don't define your life by them.

What I think is a better focus rather than success is what Bob Buford, in his book *Half Times,* calls "significance"—move from success to significance.

I think the opposite of accumulation of wealth is generosity. I wrote a book called, *The Generosity Factor* with Truett Cathy, founder of Chick-fil-A. He is one of the most generous men I've ever met in my life. I thought we needed to have a model of generosity— generosity not only with your treasure, but your time, and talent. Truett and I added *touch* as a fourth one.

The opposite of recognition is service. I think you become an adult when you realize you're here to serve rather than to be served.

Finally, the opposite of power and status is having loving relationships. Mother Theresa is a good example. She couldn't have cared less about recognition, power, and status because she was focused on generosity, service, and loving relationships. She did get all of that earthly stuff such as recognition and status; but if you focus on the earthly, such as money, recognition, and power, you're never going to get to significance. I you focus on significance, you'll be amazed at how much success can come your way.

Wright

I spoke with Truett Cathy recently and was impressed by what a down-to-earth good man he seems to be. He has Chick-fil-A close on Sundays. When my friends found out I had talked to him, they said, "Boy, he must be a great Christian man, but he's rich." I told them, "Well, to put his faith into perspective, closing on Sunday costs him $500 million a year." He lives his faith, doesn't he?

Blanchard

Absolutely, but he still outsells everybody else.

Blanchard

That's right.

Blanchard

They were recently chosen the number one fast quick service restaurant in Los Angeles. They only have five restaurants here and they've only been here for a year.

Wright

The simplest market scheme, I told him, tripped me up. I walked by the first Chick-fil-A I had ever seen, and some girl came out with chicken stuck on toothpicks and handed me one. I just grabbed it and ate it and it's history from there on.

Blanchard

Yes, I think so. It's really special. It is so important that people understand generosity, service and loving relationships because too many people are running around like a bunch of peacocks. You even see pastors who ask, "How many in your congregation are authors, how many books have you sold?" or, regarding business, "What's your profit margin? What's your sales?" The reality is, that's all well and good, but I think what you need to focus on is others. I think if businesses did that more and we got Wall Street off our backs with all the short-term evaluation, we'd be a lot better off.

Wright

Absolutely. There seems to be a clear theme that winds through many of your books that have to do with success in business and organizations and that theme is how management treats people and how they feel about their value to a company. Is this an accurate observation? If so, can you elaborate on it?

Blanchard

Yes, it's a very accurate observation. See, I think "profit" is the applause you get for taking care of your customers and creating a motivating environment for your people. Very often people believe business is only about the bottom line. But no, the bottom line happens to be the result of creating customers who are raving fans. I described this with Sheldon Bowles in our book. Customers want to brag about you, and then create an environment where people can be gung-ho and committed. You've got to take care of your customers and your people, and then your cash register is going to go ka-ching. Then is when you can make some big bucks.

Wright

I noticed that your professional title with the Ken Blanchard Companies is somewhat unique, Chairman and "Chief Spiritual Officer." What does your title mean to you personally and to your company? How does it affect the books you choose to write?

Blanchard

I remember having lunch with Max Dupree one time. He's the legendary Chairman of Herman Miller, Inc. He wrote a wonderful book called, *Leadership is an Art.* I asked him once, "What's your job?"

He said, "I basically work in the vision area."

"Well, what do you do?" I asked.

"I'm like a third grade teacher," He said, "I say our vision and values over, and over, and over again until people get it right, right, right."

I decided then I was going to become our Chief Spiritual Officer. I would be working in the vision, values, and energy part of our business. I would leave a morning message every day for everybody in our company. We have about 275 to 300 around the country, in Canada, and the U.K., and we have partners in about thirty nations. I leave a voice mail every morning, and I do three things regarding that as Chief Spiritual Officer:

1. People tell me those we need to pray for,
2. People tell me about those we need to praise—our unsung heroes and people like that and,
3. I leave an inspirational morning message every day.

I am really the cheerleader—the "energy bunny"—in our company, and the one who reminds us why we're here and what we're trying to do. Our business in the Ken Blanchard Companies is to help people to lead at a higher level, and to help individuals and organizations. Our mission statement is, "To unleash the power and potential of people and organizations for the common good." So if we are going to do that, we've really got to believe in that. I'm working on getting more Chief Spiritual Officers around the country. I think it's a great title—we should get more of them.

Wright

So those people for whom you pray, where do you get the names?

Blanchard

The people in the company tell me who needs help, whether it's a spouse who is sick, or kids who are sick, or they are worried about something. We've got more than five years of data about the power of prayer, which is pretty important.

For example, this morning my inspirational message was about my wife and five members of our company who walked sixty miles last weekend—twenty miles a day for three days—to raise money for breast cancer research. It was amazing. I went down and waved them all in as they came. There was a ceremony where it was announced they had raised 7.6 million dollars. There were more than three thousand people walking—a lot of the walkers were dressed in pink, they were cancer victors—people who had overcome cancer. There were even men who were walking with pictures of their wives who had died from breast cancer. I thought it was incredible.

There wasn't one mention of it in the major San Diego papers on Monday. I said, "Isn't that just something." I said, "We have to be an island of positive influence because you know, all you see in the paper today is about Michael Jackson and Scott Peterson and Coby Bryant and this kind of thing, when here you have all these thousands of people out there walking and trying to make a difference, and nobody thinks it's news." So every morning I pump people up about what life's about and about what's going on. That's what my Chief Spiritual Officer job is about.

Wright

I had the pleasure of reading one of your current releases, *The Leadership Pill.*

Blanchard

Yes.

Wright

I must admit that my first thought was how short the book was. I wondered if I was going to get my money's worth, which, by the way, I most certainly did. Many of your books are brief and based on a fictional story. Most business books in the market today are hundreds of pages in length and read almost like a textbook. Will you talk a little bit about why you write these short books and about the premise of *The Leadership Pill?*

Blanchard

I really got that during my relationship with Spencer Johnson when we wrote the *One Minute Manager.* As you know he wrote *Who Moved My Cheese,* which was a phenomenal success. He wrote children's books, and I was a storyteller. As I said earlier, my wife told me, "You guys ought to write a children's book for managers. They won't read anything else."

Jesus talked by parable. My favorite books were, *Jonathan Livingston Seagull, The Littlest Prince,* and *Og Mandino*—the greatest of them all. These are all great parables. I started writing parables because people can get into the story and learn the contents of the story without bringing their judgmental hats into their reading. You write a regular book and they'll say, "Well, where did you get the research?" They get into that judgmental side. Our books get them emotionally involved and they learn.

The Leadership Pill is a fun story about a pharmaceutical company convinced they have discovered the secret to leadership and that they can put the ingredients in a pill. When they announce it, the country goes crazy because everybody knows we need more effective leaders. When they release it, it outsells Viagra and all those big gray trucks. The founders of the company start selling off stock and they call them "Pillionaires."

Then along comes this guy who calls himself "the effective manager," and he challenges them to a no-pill challenge. If they identify two non-performing groups, he'll take on one and let somebody on the pill take another one, and he guarantees his group will out-perform the other group by the end of the year. They agree, but of course, they give him a drug test every week to make sure he's not sneaking pills on the side.

I wrote the book with Marc Muchnick who was a young guy in his early thirties. We did a major study together of what does this interesting "Y" generation—the young people of today—want from leaders, and this is a secret blend that this effective manager in the book uses.

When you think about it, David, this is really powerful in terms of what people want from a leader. Number one, they want integrity. Many people have talked about that in the past, but these young people will walk if they see people say one thing and do another. A lot of us walk into the bathroom and out into the halls to talk about it. But these people will quit. They don't want somebody to say something and not do it.

The second thing they want is a partnership relationship. They hate superior/subordinate. I mean, what awful terms those are. It's a case of the head of the department versus the hired hands. Someone asks, "What do you do?" The reply is, "I'm in supervision—I see things a lot clearer than these stupid idiots." They want to be treated as partners. If they can get a financial partnership, that's great. I if they can't, they really want at least a psychological partnership where they can bring their brains to work and make decisions.

Then finally, they want affirmation. They not only want to be caught doing things right, but they want to be affirmed for who they are. They want to be known as a person, not as a number.

So those are the three ingredients this effective manager in the story uses. They are wonderful values if you think of them. Rank order values for any organization is number one: integrity. In our company we call it "ethics"—our number one value. Number two value is partnership. Partnership in our companies is relationships. Number three is affirmation—being affirmed as a human being. I think that ties into relationships, too. They are wonderful values that can drive behavior in a great way.

Wright

I believe most people in today's business culture would agree that success in business has everything to do with successful leadership. In *The Leadership Pill*, you present a simple but profound premise that being in leadership is not something you do *to* people; it's something you do *with* them. At face value, that seems incredibly obvious, but you must have found in your research and in your observations that leaders in today's culture do not get this. Would you speak to that issue?

Blanchard

Yes. I think what often happens is this is the human ego, you know. There are too many leaders out there who are self-serving. They're not serving leaders. They think the sheep are there for the benefit of the shepherd. All the power, money, and famous recognition all reside at the top of the hierarchy. They forget that the real action in business is not at the top, it's in the one-to-one, moment-to-moment interactions your front line people have with your customers, it's how the phone was answered, how problems are dealt with, and those kinds of things. If you don't think you're doing leadership *with* them, rather than *to* them, after a while they won't take care of your customers.

I was at a store recently, it's not Nordstrom's where I normally would go, and I thought of something I had to share with my wife, Margie. I asked the guy behind the counter in the Men's Wear Department, "May I use your phone?"

He said, "No," rather emphatically.

I said, "You're kidding me. I can always use the phone at Nordstrom's."

He said, "Look, buddy, they won't let *me* use the phone here, why should I let *you* use the phone?"

That is an example of leadership that's done to them not with them. People want a partnership. People want to be involved in a way that really makes a difference.

Wright

Dr. Blanchard, the time has flown by and there are so many more questions I'd like to ask you. In conclusion, would you mind sharing with our readers some closing thoughts on success? If you were mentoring a small group of men and women, and one of their central goals was to become successful, what kind of advice would you give them?

Blanchard

I would first of all ask, "What are you focused on?" As I said earlier, I think if you are focused on success as being accumulation of money, recognition, power, or status, I think you've got the wrong target.

What you need to really be focused on is how can you be generous in the use of your time, your talent, your treasure, and touch. How can you serve people rather than be served? How can you develop caring, loving relationships with people? My sense is if you will focus on those things, success in the traditional sense will come to you. But if you go out and say, "Man, I'm going to make a fortune, and I'm going to do this," whatever it may be and if you focus on those kinds of things, you might even get some of those numbers. You become an adult, however, when you realize you are here to give rather than to get. You're here to serve not to be served. I would just say to people, that life is such a very special occasion. Don't miss it by aiming at a target that bypasses other people, because we're really here to serve each other. That's what I would share with people.

Wright

Well, what an enlightening conversation, Dr. Blanchard. I really want you to know how much I appreciate all the time you've taken with me for this interview. I know that our readers will learn from this, and I really appreciate your being with us today.

Blanchard

Well, thank you so much, David. I really enjoyed my time with you. You've asked some great questions that made me think. I hope my answers are helpful to other people because, as I say, life is a special occasion.

Wright

Today we have been talking with Dr. Ken Blanchard, author of the phenomenal best selling book, *The One Minute Manager*. The fact that he's the "Chief Spiritual Officer" of his company should give us all cause to think about how we are leading our companies and leading our families and leading anything, whether it is within church or civic organizations. I know I will.

Thank you so much, Dr. Blanchard, for being with us today on *Masters of Success.*

Blanchard

Good to be with you, David.

About The Author

Few people have created more of a positive impact on the day-to-day management of people and companies than Dr. Kenneth Blanchard, who is known around the world simply as "Ken." When Ken speaks, he speaks from the heart with warmth and humor. His unique gift is to speak to an audience and communicate with each individual as if they were alone and talking one-on-one. He is a polished storyteller with a knack for making the seemingly complex easy to understand. Ken has been a guest on a number of national television programs, including Good Morning America and The Today Show, and has been featured in *Time, People, U.S. News & World Report*, and a host of other popular publications. He earned his bachelor's degree in government and philosophy from Cornell University, his master's degree in sociology and counseling from Colgate University, and his Ph.D. in educational administration and leadership from Cornell University.

Dr. Ken Blanchard

The Ken Blanchard Companies

125 State Place

Escondido, California 92029

Phone: 800-728-6000

Fax: 760-489-8407

www.blanchardtraining.com

Chapter Three

COLLEEN KETTENHOFEN

David Wright (Wright)

Today we are speaking with Colleen Kettenhofen. She is an international speaker and author and has spoken before thousands in forty-seven states and six countries including, Ireland, England, Scotland, Wales, and Canada. She specializes in improving communication, public speaking, leadership, management skills, team building, wellness, and success.

After graduating from Southern Methodist University Colleen assumed a sales position where she was later honored as the number one sales "superstar" in the history of the company. Combining this with her advertising executive years, Colleen speaks from experience when it comes to sharing powerful leadership skills.

Colleen, welcome to *Masters of Success*.

Colleen Kettenhofen (Kettenhofen)

Thank you.

Wright

So how did you begin speaking and why did you choose strategies for success, leadership and public speaking as your main topics?

Kettenhofen

My background is in sales (where I did a lot of public speaking) and also management. What I really enjoyed about previous jobs was that "customer connection," when I would deliver a presentation or meet with them one-on- one. After years of winning sales awards I started my own training business, chose success, leadership and public speaking as my main topics. I wanted to share with others the proven strategies I had used to become successful. With my company, we have a strong commitment to helping people learn basic but necessary skills both personally and professionally. The beauty of these time-tested secrets is that you can apply them to any area and almost be *guaranteed* of immediate results. Some of these areas include setting and achieving goals, increasing your income, dealing with a difficult person or employee, overcoming negativity, improving teamwork, and overcoming nervousness when delivering a presentation.

For example, it's amazing how at the end of my public speaking workshops how noticeable it is to everyone how much someone has improved in their presentation skills. Self-confidence skyrockets and morale is boosted. When you study success what you're really studying is psychology. Anybody can be successful if they put their mind to it because I believe it's all in the mind.

Also, a big part of success in life is effective communication and learning to get along with others. I find it interesting that my most requested programs are "Dealing with Difficult People," "Dealing with Difficult Employees" and "how to handle a hostile audience" when I speak on "Improving Your Presentation Skills". All these topics make a difference in becoming more successful and enhancing your career.

Wright

What is the main message you want people to hear so they can learn from your success?

Kettenhofen

That you will have trials and tribulations, but that you can learn lessons from them, and emerge better and stronger. I am a cancer survivor (15 years and going strong!) and I lost my mother at a young age. When you go through challenging times, you are forced to grow and are stretched out of your comfort zone. I think of each trial as a lesson plan and life as the study guide. And I believe that if you want to be more successful, especially in business, you have to "stretch" out of your comfort zone. It's often said that your comfort zone is your money zone.

Wright

My wife is a cancer survivor, my hats off to all you folks.

Kettenhofen

Oh really? What type?

Wright

Colorectal.

Kettenhofen

That's what I had. Luckily, it was stage zero, the earliest stage.

Early detection is key. I wrote an article about it on my Web site in terms of how a diagnosis like this actually changes your life for the better. When I do my programs, initially people will often complain about their jobs. Then, if I decide to "weave" my experience into the presentation, suddenly you can hear a pin drop. It puts everything into perspective for them and serves as a wake-up call. It makes me seem more human to them; they suddenly sit up in their seats and listen to everything.

Wright

So in your seminars, keynotes, CDs, and on your Web site, do you suggest ways organizations and individuals can handle these problems related to dealing with difficult people, overcoming procrastination, improving your public speaking skills and becoming more successful?

Kettenhofen

Yes, if it's a live speaking engagement, one crucial thing I do way ahead of time is to do a lot of *listening* and *interviewing*. I find out who's going to be in the audience and what their expectations are. I interview people, find out what their goals and objectives are going into the program and take notes.

During the program, I give everyone real-world examples and proven-to-work strategies based on the most up-to-the-minute research. I ask them to put a specific action plan into writing. Action and accountability are key. They often report later that they've seen immediate results.

Wright

So, is this what makes your perspective unique?

Kettenhofen

Yes, and based on what clients are saying, 3 things make this perspective unique 1) Having conducted almost one thousand speaking engagements in forty-seven states and 6 countries, day in and day out, I hear what people's greatest challenges are, what works and what doesn't. 2) Having been in the business world for 24 years, I've been in their shoes, I've lived it, whether in management, sales, or just in understanding the importance of excellent communication skills. And 3) the programs are interactive, informative and <u>fun</u>. The live programs often involve some paired and group activities along with colorful slides. When people are entertained, they *retain* the information better.

Wright

So how does your unique perspective improve an individual's or an employee's productivity?

Kettenhofen

First, the emphasis is on accountability, action plans and personal responsibility. I give guaranteed, time-tested easy techniques participants can apply *that very same day*. Based on years of experience, I've really listened and focused in on what people's greatest challenges are such as overcoming procrastination, overcoming negativity in the workplace, or how to increase productivity. Afterwards, people often report to me their successes, and how much more "in control" of their circumstances they feel. Their attitudes become more positive.

Wright

What do you see as one of the key problems or challenges organizations face in today's climate and how can these challenges be resolved?

Kettenhofen

What I hear about over and over is "lack of communication, trust," and more specifically, "lack of conflict resolution skills," which leads to decreased productivity and lower morale. One thing I see is many people are promoted to leadership and management positions because they possess the "hard skills" or technical skills but often have no formal training in "people skills" communication, or how to handle conflict. So I'm often called in to train individuals in leadership positions or on teams, about the importance of communication. However, in my programs, I ask *them* to list what traits they think are important for a leader, manager or team to be successful. That's when they often say, "people skills."

This way, it's as though it was their idea. You can see the lights going on in their heads by the end of the workshop.

I know this will sound basic, but truly, the biggest challenge I see in most organizations is a breakdown in communication. For example, often a manager or supervisor will have "inherited" a difficult employee. They don't know how to really give that individual constructive feedback without putting the employee on the defensive. One of the main reasons managers don't address performance problems is they want to avoid conflict. Also, a lot of managers and supervisors will tell me privately that they know they should document but that they don't. They say they "don't have the time." I reiterate to everyone in my management and leadership programs how and what to document with a difficult employee and why it is so imperative.

Wright

Every time I ask this next question I get about as many answers as people I ask, but I'm going to do it anyway. How do you define success?

Kettenhofen

Success is an attitude. It is a skill and the best part is it can be learned. Success is not necessarily having lots of money because that doesn't always bring happiness. Yet, success does afford you the freedom to do things you enjoy such as an Alaska cruise - my personal favorite, or a trip to an island or mountain resort, or just spending time with family. I think successful people discipline themselves to do things that others don't want to do. They have a good attitude no matter what happens to them, are able to turn a negative into a positive, and also possess the ability to see long term. Because of that they have a better grasp on delaying gratification. Success is overall fulfillment and happiness as opposed to short-term fun.

Wright

What would you say has been the biggest contribution to your professional success?

Kettenhofen

It's a combination of things. The books I read, seminars and conferences I attend, along with audio programs, plus being surrounded by supportive people. It's also sheer determination and passion for what I do as well as spiritual beliefs. Every morning I ask for guidance, and then take action on that guidance. It is one of the things that helps tremendously and is an excellent investment of time.

Wright

You know, a man I like and appreciate very much told me many, many years ago that his definition of a rut was "a grave with both ends kicked out." You talk a lot about how often people are stuck in a rut, so how do you suggest others get started on the path to personal and professional success?

Kettenhofen

Begin by finding your passion. When you love what you do, it's not work, it energizes you.

Here's another tip. I read that the average car owner spends 500 to 1,000 hours per year in his/her car. Everyone's busy so it's important to make time to listen to CDs in your car. Learn to multi-task more effectively. Attend seminars and conferences that interest you so that you can surround yourself with people you want as role models and mentors. Be with the right people—those who are supportive of your dream. Because if you're stuck and you suddenly discover your passion, you want to be with people who will support your dream not tear it down. Read books that motivate and inspire you, especially that first hour and last hour of the day when your mind is most amenable to suggestion. Start with baby steps. Do *something*, do anything that will bring you closer to your goal every day because those action steps will be compounded over time. Expect roadblocks because there *will* be roadblocks. Just practice patience, diligence, and faith. *Don't ever give up!*

Wright

What an interesting conversation. I'm learning a lot—I always do— is there more of this type of information available from you?

Kettenhofen

Yes, this information is in greater detail on my Web site at www.ColleenSpeaks.com. There we feature free articles offering advice on topics such as "How to Overcome Procrastination," "Dealing with Difficult People," "Million-Dollar Mindsets" parts 1 and 2, "Top Foods to Boost Your Mood," "How to Increase Your Energy and Enthusiasm," "The Leadership Test," "Dealing with Difficult Employees: 9 Facts You Must Document," and other related subjects for people who want this information immediately. There's also an electronic newsletter and free audio programs on topics such as how to set goals and get what you want, increase your income, achieve peak performance personally and professionally. So our customers find it very useful. And we are *constantly* updating and enhancing the information.

Wright

Thank you, Colleen, for taking so much time to speak with us and help us understand.

Kettenhofen

Thank you, David.

Wright

Today, we've been talking with Colleen Kettenhofen. She is an international speaker and author. After graduating from Southern Methodist University she assumed a sales position where she was later honored as the number one sales "superstar" in the history of the company at Holt, Rinehart and Winston. Along with her management and advertising executive years, she speaks from experience, as we have found out here today. When it comes to sharing powerful leadership skills we now know what they are talking about.

Thank you so much, Colleen, for being with us today.

Kettenhofen

Thank *you*, David.

About The Author

An international speaker, Colleen Kettenhofen has spoken in forty-seven states and six countries: Ireland, Scotland, England, Wales, and Canada. She specializes in improving communication, public speaking, dealing with difficult people, leadership and management development, team building, wellness, and success with an emphasis on accountability and action plans. As a former number one sales producer for a Fortune 500 company as well as her management years, Colleen shares her secrets with thousands.

Colleen Kettenhofen

Colleen Kettenhofen and Associates, LLC

Phone: 1.800.323.0683

Phone: 971.212-2412

www.ColleenSpeaks.com

Chapter Four

NICK CONNER

THE INTERVIEW

David E. Wright (Wright)

Today we're talking with Nicholas D. Conner. Nicholas is head of program development and the owner of TeamBuilders, one of this country's foremost training and development companies specializing in team performance development as well as leadership development. Over the past eighteen years his consultative relationships have included small businesses to Fortune Twenty companies.

His program designs range from coaching for effective teams to high performance team synergy workshops as well as self-managed work teams. His unique technique of creating interactive workshops using action learning in conjunction with measurement and assessment tools provides not just insights but more importantly, the applications for personal and team growth.

He has written and provided information for several publications including *American Executive* magazine, *Training and Development (T+D)* magazine, and *Corporate & Incentive Travel* magazine to name a few. You can find him passionately sharing his experiences at industry specific conferences on high performance teams and leadership. He also specializes in the use of the Myers-Briggs Type

Indicator®, the Leadership Practices Inventory, and TeamBuilders' own FiveSTAR Team Performance Indicator®.

Nicholas is a member of the National Speakers Association, the American Society for Training and Development, the Association for Experiential Education, the Northwest Human Resource Association, and the University of Florida Alumni New England Gator Club.

Nick, welcome to *Masters of Success*.

Nicholas D. Conner (Conner)

Thank you, David. It's good to be here.

Wright

So, how do you define a successful, high performance team?

Conner

The definition of a high performance team really depends on the team itself. Definitions can vary, but for example, if you and I are on the same team, we need to be aligned with a common definition. Therefore, all of our skills, actions, decisions, and behaviors are complementary of one another. To answer your question, *a team is members of a diverse group of people who struggle for shared aspirations (a common goal) with measurable performance and accountability.* Achieving goals is the easy part. Achieving goals within a fine balance of the task, process and people involved...well, that's high performance. The attributes or core competencies within this definition include a trusting environment that promotes candor, conflict, and commitment to the common goal. All actions, decisions, and behaviors must be made with that team's focus on its sense of purpose and objectives.

Wright

So, how do you define leadership?

Conner

Again, there are varying definitions. Leadership is an art. As leaders we are challenged with getting our teams to want to do, want to be, and want to perform their best at the highest level of commitment. This includes understanding the "why's" of their business and sharing in the outcomes. To connect these definitions, in order for leadership to support and motivate a team, they must be clear what a team is.

Wright

There are many companies out there today that are doing team-building and your client list reads like a Who's Who of global business. How is it that they choose to partner with you?

Conner

There are a lot of outstanding experts in the field of Team Development and you can tell the difference. There is a difference between the varying levels of team-building and team development. There are recreational team-building programs that may include corporate olympics or raft building, which focus more on socialization. Although they are fun, no real epiphanies about the group and its business will take place. "Team building" is a lot like the word "teams" in that we use them both as a positive motivating title. Team development programs have more meat on the bone. Whether we are part of a large annual conference or working with interactive work groups, team development programs must be performance based and results driven.

Unfortunately, team building has become almost a cliché in business because of all the different types of recreational based programs and "just for fun" programs out there. The activities in any team development program will surface insights about a group, its individuals, or the business in general. The key is to take these insights and create momentum or create a plan for application. Include metrics and now we can track performance development, deliver results, and hold team members accountable.

You may have noticed that I sometimes use the word "team" and sometimes I use the word "group." They are *not* interchangeable. Teams fall under the definition we provided, whereas groups might be a nebulous cluster of people who work together.

That's why our clients have chosen us—we don't just have a lot of fun, we ask the tough questions like, "What are we going to do differently on Monday morning based on what we have experienced here together today?" Otherwise it's just an event—it truly needs to be part of a process. Our clients realize that this is what they're striving for, and that's why they invite us to design and implement programs for them.

Wright

I'm familiar with Myers-Briggs; I've also taken the DiSC several times. So what you're saying is that, rather than just a packaged team-building program, you go into the particulars of a specific team, i.e., how are we going to change based on what we've just learned from these assessments, right?

Conner

Actually, all programs have to be customized because each organization and each team operates in different cultures with different needs and different desired outcomes. Not every program design includes measurement or assessment.

Personality indicators like the Myers-Briggs Type Indicator, DiSC, and the Belbin Team Roles, are more subjective types of instruments. These are more about awareness and understanding, but to address your question—how does knowing one is a high D (DiSC), an Intuitive (MBTI), or a Shaper (Belbin), effect the way we function as a team—there must be an application to this newfound awareness. Go back to our definition of a team and we reference the diversity and skills of the team's members.

The other types of instruments that are more measurable would be something like the Leadership Practices Inventory (LPI) or the FiveSTAR Team Performance Indicator. These tools are quantitative. They are the metrics providing diagnostic data a well as measurement for performance. "Team building," for example, has always been so intangible. The programs themselves—ROPES courses, cognitive activities, or Edventure pursuits—are commodities. They provide concrete objectives in which the group is put in a situation of perceived risk, real time deadlines, stress, or fear. Successful completion of these objectives is a collective effort. The discussion afterwards will surface the insights for better performance.

Results are the product and metrics provide the measurement and tracking of success. The LPI, for example, provides 360-degree feedback (even though it is perception of leadership) so a customized design is rolled out to, again, surface insights and action plan and measure application.

The FiveSTAR Team Performance Indicator will provide data on a group's level of trust, level of communication, conflict, role clarity, vision, and it will also tell us what stage of development it is functioning within. If we know this, we can then design a program that will address those issues and then follow up with the instrument down the road to see if they are actually making progress and being held accountable for their actions.

FiveSTAR TPI
Team Performance Indicator

Wright

Since success is the subject here, what is your success model for developing leaders in teams in business?

Conner

Again, it depends on the group itself and how they are defining purpose and performance—what are we committed to accomplishing? When we design our programs we do an in-depth needs assessment. We need to understand the dynamics of the group, the culture of the organization, and how they are defining success. Performance of the team's development must be measurable as well.

We very often take the Stephen Covey *(The Seven Habits of Highly Effective People)* approach of "beginning with the end in mind," and ask our clients, "If this is a 'home run'—if we do an absolutely perfect job—what's it look like to you?" If they can define that for us, then we can work from the end, go back to the beginning, and start filling in blanks on how to achieve these goals. We may advise on measurement or assessment. The program design could vary between more cognitive types of activities or somewhat physical or adventurous (*regardless, no program is about physical dexterity or athletics*). The more results driven programs will require strategic action planning for performance measures.

We have to make sure that what we design is part of a larger process. We need to know how this fits into their business plan and the group's common purpose. It can't just be a one-shot, "boy, I hope this works" kind of thing (*hope is not a plan*). We have to walk away, not just feeling good about this thing, but also with a course of action in hand. So, at the end of the day, the tough questions were asked, insights were surfaced, and actions established to be implemented.

For example, during a debrief we asked three types of questions: "What?" which refers to the assessment or the activity; "So what?" What does this have to do with us, as individuals, as a group, and our performance goals; "Now what?" What are we going to do differently, how will I change as we move forward down the road, and how do we hold each other accountable?

Wright

I'm encouraged that, unlike many people who teach and train, you do interactive sessions. Do you mean ropes courses and things like that?

Conner

Ropes courses are a form of interactive learning. It's a small part of our business. Again, we begin with the end in mind—and if a particular client needs a great, climactic ending maybe we'll include a high level activity; but most of our programs are along the lines of cognitive activities that allow us to watch the groups' dynamics, draw metaphors, and ask questions. We call them "Mobile Learning Initiatives." These are activities we can do at any venue—indoors or outdoors, anywhere around the world. These activities, in fact, actually do a better job providing us group dynamics. As I stated earlier our programs are not about physical dexterity, or athleticism, unless our client desires it and the needs assessment shows a fit.

We operate on what we call a "full choice philosophy." What that basically means is, regardless of whether they're non-physical or even the more physically adventurous types of programs, folks choose the degree in which they want to be challenged—that is their decision. There are clients who have different physical limitations such as bad knees or bad backs, hypertension, and even emotional things going on.

Getting out of your comfort zone may mean climbing thirty feet in the air but it also may mean introverts speaking their mind or an extroverted person holding back a bit and listening to someone else.

"Interactive" doesn't necessarily mean a thirty-foot-in-the-air ropes course type of activity. "Interactive" means that folks are engaged in some capacity. It's not a talking head in front of the room telling groups, "Here's what a high performance team should be." It's about groups experiencing it. Going back to our debrief, they discuss the What, they discuss the So-what, and they get busy on the Now-what.

Wright

When I picture the ropes courses and things like that I think immediately that this stuff has been around for a while and hasn't it all been done before? What do you think?

Conner

Well, that question comes up a lot, even from some of our team members. For example, we sometimes need to remind ourselves that just because we use activities over and over again, whether it's the more cognitive or the physical stuff, this is new to a lot of our participants. Also, an older type of activity can be framed and debriefed differently. A lot of it depends on the skill of the facilitator to extract applicable metaphor and meaning.

But you've brought up a very good point. When Kurt Hahn founded Outward Bound in 1941, ropes courses used to be called "confidence courses." They have been around for quite some time. Many of our clients are asking us what else is out there? They have experienced ropes courses. They'll say, "We liked them, they were pretty cool, but what else is out there that is interactive?" We do have a variety of things to offer such as the Mobile Learning Initiatives, which can be taken on the road. We have a program called "Pursuit" which is actually focused on GPSs and the sport of geocaching, which is fascinating. If you have not tried it yet, I highly recommend it. Participants love using technology with their exploration.

What interactive learning does is allow us to see group dynamics in a controlled situation. "Launching the Future" is a fun yet powerful program of ours that is focused on the Leadership Practices Inventory survey by Kouzes & Posner and discusses the early years of the space program, which has wonderful examples of the Leadership Practices. We discuss John F. Kennedy, Apollo XIII, and all the exemplary leadership that took place.

One of the highlights for me was when I was a speaker at a Launching the Future program with Commander James Lovell. It was so amazing to share the stage with him and discuss the Leadership Practices of the Apollo Mission with a hero who echoed our points with his first-hand experience.

Other programs include "Mission Possible" and "Rube Goldberg" types of sessions that are very fun and tangible types of interactive workshops.

Groups can also participate in some more philanthropic types of projects. We sometimes have our clients paint some houses, or build a handicapped access ramp, or put a playground in a park. We'll get to do something in the community and still get to see the group dynamics for debrief. It really doesn't matter what the activity is.

See, David, the activities are not teambuilding in and of themselves—a talented facilitator extracts applicable metaphors (not one-size-fits-all generic metaphors) from each activity, which creates the prompt for discussion. It's this candid discussion that drives at the issues of the group (what, so what, now what?)

For example, when we are asked, "Hey, I need to build trust in my team. What activities do you have that build trust?"

We'll say, "Well, we don't have any." It's kind of a tongue-in-cheek reply but true.

They'll say, "What do you mean? We have heard of trust falls, trust walks—aren't those trust building exercises?"

Actually the answer is no. The truth is we do have activities that will surface the issues of trust, but if you want to build trust—be trustworthy. Building trust is process—a process that might include better communication, reliability, respect, or any action that supports the group's purpose and performance. The same can be said for respect, by the way. If you want to be respected, be respectful.

Wright

Will you tell our readers about the measurement and assessment part of team development programs?

Conner

Sure. We actually touched on it earlier. There are some qualitative assessment tools—the Myers-Briggs Type Indicator is a wonderful tool—it's one of our favorites; Belbin Team Roles is a unique tool that

I learned about while partnering on some programs in the U.K., and some folks prefer DiSC. All of these instruments are very good at creating awareness and understanding that there are diverse roles we all play within a team based on what can be described as strengths and weaknesses.

Up close they all are attributes of our type or style, but we must remember that every action has an equal and opposite reaction. In other words, for everything we are very good at there is always something we are not very good at. That's why these complimentary skills and functions are so important to a team. To another type or style our strengths can be perceived as our weaknesses. Why? Because it's not the way I would have done it. So these tools are excellent for helping team members better communicate, tap into intellectual diversity, and have a clearer understanding that, just because it's different it's not wrong, but it could be complementary.

Regarding the Myers-Briggs Type Indicator. I'm an INTP, for example, and the joke around the MBTI industry is that we INTPs are our biggest fans. INTPs have what can be defined as "competency issues" with other team members. In other words, "no one does it better than I do." As a result though, I found myself on a lot of airplanes doing a lot of team and leadership development programs myself. Understanding the dynamics of my MBTI and with a little help from Michael Gerber, author of *The E Myth Revisited*, I realized that I needed to continue to develop our product (not *be* the product) and to develop our talented team of facilitators if TeamBuilders was to grow and accomplish its aggressive goals. All of this meant that I, as an INTP, needed to let go and trust. That's the beauty of the application.

Today, performance development is about results: "How do I know it's working?" "If a higher functioning team is going to impact my ROI how then do you measure the group's development?" This is where the metrics driven tools such as the Leadership Practices Inventory and the FiveSTAR Team Performance Indicator come in. This is when we want to actually be able to measure and track development.

All training really should have a level of measurement to it. We've incorporated measurement into team development, which historically has been an intangible commodity. The reason I refer to it as a commodity is because the ROPES course and any activities—even the assessment tools—are just "stuff." The learning and application and the success that comes from it is the product. It's one thing to qualitatively walk away feeling good about the progress of your group; having an action plan supported by data is another.

One particular example, for instance, is a team leader who was concerned that her team was stuck in a forming stage because of some recent change. Team members were very dependent on leadership for direction and role clarity and as a result of the uncertainty of change there were some significant trust issues, which the FiveSTAR TPI data supported. She needed to accelerate her team's development and get the team to establish its norms, a common purpose, and create some momentum for performance. The FiveStar TPI was used as a diagnostic to help us design the series of programs and give this group a starting point.

In our first session we discussed results with the group just as we would any activity focusing on what, so what and (of course) now what? If a group's data shows a trust score, for example, of a 2.5 team, we need to start describing what a 3.0 team looks like. We also need to provide the actions that are going to help the team get there and track the team's progress.

The FiveStar's five competencies are: role clarity, vision, communication, trust, and problem-solving. It will also determine a group's stage of development, which may be: dependency, conflict, cohesion, interdependency, and/or self-managing/self-directing. We also need to understand fully that self-management or self-directed work teams may not be an objective of that group. If that is the case, those scores should be extremely low and it should be a non-issue. The fact is we do need teams before we can even consider self-managed teams.

Wright

What are some of the business scenarios that would motivate an organization to seek out your skills?

Conner

There are a few different scenarios. One of the most common is when a merger and acquisition has taking place. Several cultures—at least two, if not more—are now coming together as one. That creates a lot of very interesting dynamics. We may be brought in as a catalyst to help move them from point A to point B in a very accelerated fashion.

Change is one of the things that is a constant factor in business. Organizations come to us and we design a series of programs to get them to their desired outcomes. We will then follow up and consult with them through the rest of the process as needed.

One of the keys to a successful program is to manage expectations. What I mean is that a one- or two-day program is not going to create a high performance team. If anything, it creates awareness, it creates understanding, and with a sound action plan it will create application to move the group forward. The programs themselves are not an event—they should be part of a process.

One of our fortés is when clients ask us to be part of an annual meeting. Sometimes we are the keynotes and sometimes a high profile speaker is brought in like Jim Lovell, commander of Apollo XIII, for example. At that event, using the Leadership Practices as our learning foundation, we were able to connect examples from the early space program and the Apollo mission. It was a beautiful fit. After the speaker's presentation, we moved into breakouts for interactive activities throughout the day. After the activities the participants came back and we provided a talk show format where the CEO of the company and I sat on bar stools on stage and had a candid conversation about the day. We revisited all the activities, all the metaphors, and transferred the learning back to their business.

This is becoming a very common format for team-builders to use with large types of conferences and meetings. Of course, with an officer of the company on stage it really establishes credibility and application for that organization.

And, of course, we are brought in when there is some dysfunctional activity going on with a specific team. In these types of programs we will need to roll up our sleeves and "dig at some cavities." We may open up some cans of worms, but we need enough time to put the lid back on and get some processes in place so that the group can actually move forward.

Sometimes programs are designed for a one-shot momentum builder. Others are extended commitments as a year-long or a two-year process. Self-managed work teams are an excellent example. First, we need to build a team and then we can define the roles and responsibilities associated with this drastic change. Everyone's role changes—especially leaders' roles.

Wright

You really peaked my interest when you started talking about turning insights into applications. What does that mean exactly?

Conner

I think that experiential learning, interactive learning, or action learning—whatever we want to call it—historically has done an outstanding job at surfacing insights. Participants walk away thinking, "Hmm. That was pretty cool." But then, that's where it ends. Groups go back to the office and it's "business as usual." Groups need to shift their paradigms and go back to work with a "business as *un*usual" mentality. Again, what are we going to be doing differently on Monday morning as a result of our time together? Those are the applications! Otherwise it was just a fun day together. There's quite a difference between spending money and investing it.

Wright

So how do you know which components to add when customizing programs for different clients?

Conner

It goes back to that Stephen Covey approach—beginning with the end in mind. It comes from conversation(s)—the in-depth needs assessment. Whether we utilize the FiveSTAR TPI as a pre-program diagnostic tool, interview the group leader, or interview the whole group, once we gather information we then define what a perfect session looks like with its objectives and desired outcomes. Then we go back to the beginning and start adding the components that will make it all happen.

Wright

There are many people out there who will contest that team-building programs simply just don't work. So, why do they fail?

Conner

For all the reasons that you and I just spoke about—nothing changed when they went back. It's not just team building, there are a lot of different types of training—even in-house training—that folks will call "the flavor of the month." Those will also fail if nothing changes and if there is no follow-through. Something has to change—there has to be momentum—there has to be a process in place.

That's also why it's important to find out from our client how this team's development program fits into their business model—what are we trying to accomplish here?

There are a lot of critics out there, and rightfully so. Unfortunately people's knee jerk thoughts are of a "Kum Ba Yah" singing, tree experience. If I had a dollar for every "Kum Ba Yah" joke I'd be in Hawaii golfing every day (maybe not but you get my point). As in any industry there are folks who are very good at what they do, and some who are not. George Carlin once said while hosting *Saturday Night Live* in the '70s, "Somewhere is the world's worse doctor...and someone has a 9:00 A.M. appointment with him tomorrow." I guess that's pretty true of everything.

From a distance, it all looks the same, then you start looking at price points and say to yourself, "These guys do team-building and those guys do team-building, why does one charge $45 per person and the other is $500 per person? It all looks like team-building to me." It's not! Remember, the activities are not "team-building" in and of themselves.

Wright

As I mentioned, I'm familiar with the DiSC programs and Myers-Briggs, Action Learning, and Edventure Pursuits, but I'm not familiar with something you have designed—the FiveSTAR Team Performance Indicator. Will you explain that to me?

Conner

There are tools that will measure team development or stages of team development. The FiveSTAR was designed as a result of direct feedback from our clients asking us to make something intangible, tangible.

The FiveSTAR is an online assessment that provides data on five core competencies crucial for team performance. We collect data on a group's understanding of its role clarity and its vision—or sense of purpose—effectiveness of its communication, the trust level among one another, and the group's ability to problem-solve. It also provides information on the team's stage of development that it is functioning within. This information is very helpful when designing a program so that we know what we are dealing with and what we need to address to progress forward.

Once the FiveSTAR is debriefed with the group and insights are surfaced from the activities, performance plans can be created and followed up by administering the instrument again down the road to track progress and accountability for their actions or lack thereof.

The FiveSTAR was born as a direct result of responding to our client's input and their needs.

Wright

Nick, I really appreciate your taking this much time with me today. I've learned a lot and I'm going to talk with you more about the FiveSTAR Team Performance Indicator. It sounds like something I might be interested in.

Conner

Thanks, David. We're very pleased with the way the FiveSTAR TPI has assisted our clients in inspiring their leaders and developing their teams.

Wright

Today we've been talking with Nicholas D. Conner who is the head of program development and owner of TeamBuilders; a training and development company that provides sophisticated leadership and team development. His unique technique of creating interactive workshops using action learning with measurement and assessment provides insights as well as applications. I think we've found out here today he knows a lot about what he's talking about.

Nick, thank you so much for being with us today on *Masters of Success*.

Conner

My pleasure, David. Thank you so much.

About The Author

Nicholas D. Conner is the head of program development and owner of TeamBuilders. Over the past eighteen years his consultative relationships have included small businesses to Fortune 20 companies. He has written or been interviewed for several publications including *American Executive Magazine, Training & Development Magazine, Corporate & Incentive Travel Magazine* and he is asked to speak at industry specific conferences on leadership and high performance teams. He also specializes in the use of The Myers-Briggs Type Indicator, the Leadership Practices Inventory and TeamBuilders' own FiveStar Team Performance Indicator. He believes results-driven program designs include activity, measurement, and execution!

Nicholas D. Conner

TeamBuilders

In Florida:

35246 U.S. Highway 19 North

Palm Harbor, FL. 34684

Phone: 800-446-1172

In New England:

3 Donnelly Dr.

Medfield, MA. 02052

Phone: 508-359-1792

www.teambuilders.com

Chapter Five

SAM SLAY

THE INTERVIEW

David Wright (Wright)

Today we're speaking with Sam Slay. Sam has twenty-four years of government experience. He has also owned and operated several retail and service businesses. He's a retired chief of police; he has worked as chief of field operations, and later as a vice president of sales and marketing for a national wireless Internet company.

His opportunity to manage personnel has been both challenging and rewarding. He recognizes the power of people and the power of enthusiasm. Sam is a speaker, coach, and consultant. He is focused on effective supervisory skills, and working with employees to promote productivity and create a positive work environment. His goal is to obtain a greater Return On Investment (ROI) from staff.

Sam is the president of the Bay County Domestic Violence Task Force. He believes family violence is a national epidemic. Sam is also the owner of Sam Slay & Associates, a company providing Speaking, Coaching, and Consulting services. He is president and CEO of 357 Solutions, LLC, providing employee and organizational development.

Sam, welcome to *Masters of Success*.

Sam Slay (Slay)

Thank you, good to be here.

Wright

So, how did you get interested in personnel management and employee performance?

Slay

Early on, first as a supervisor and later as an administrator, I realized that employees are undervalued. They are a company's greatest and most undervalued assets.

Wright

So you see the company wrapped up in the value of its people.

Slay

Sometimes we think technology will take over and we fail to appreciate the value of the people operating that technology.

Wright

What are some common mistakes employees and supervisors make when working with others?

Slay

Often supervisors fail to realize employees bring additional experience and backgrounds to work from other jobs or other experiences, including individual life experience themselves. Supervisors undervalue personnel in their organizations and it happens all too frequently.

Wright

Are there any specific things you can share with me that they might do to show how they undervalue employees?

Slay

We often think of the term "micromanagement" as a bad thing. I don't believe it's a bad thing when it's initiated early and then removed once the manager has determined what the employee is able to accomplish based on general training—on the job training and formal training, etc. For some managers, the transition between micromanaging and being able to empower and delegate to employees is very difficult. That's probably the number one way a manager will undervalue an employee.

Wright

One of the reasons I work for myself is that down through the years bosses would tell me the job to be done and then start telling me how to do it—never letting me use my own creativity and imagination. It was really a negative factor for me.

Slay

It is a negative factor for a lot of people, especially people who enjoy their employment and are motivated to perform. The thought that they're not going to make mistakes is faulty thinking. The question is how much calculated risk is an organization able to withstand? At that point they are able to delegate and empower their people to accomplish more.

Wright

What single piece of advice would you give a new supervisor?

Slay

If they don't get anything else about supervision out of our conversation or this book, the number one thing is to look at their current and past supervisors, see what they are doing or have done wrong—their philosophy and the manner in which they're doing their job—and don't do that.

Wright

Are managers and supervisors adequately prepared for their new roles?

Slay

In the majority of cases I would have to say no. Sometimes it's the organization's fault. I'd say it's fifty-fifty—half the time it's the organization's fault and half the time it's the individual's fault by not personally preparing themselves. Ultimately both the employee and the organization lose. On average, or probably more than average, supervisors and managers are not prepared for their roles.

Wright

In the companies I worked for down through the years, the way to become, for example, the sales manager was to be the best salesman in the organization. A salesperson would progress in sales and finally he or she would be promoted into a job they couldn't or didn't want to do.

Slay

That's a perfect example of someone who works, for example, on an assembly line. They would do an incredible job but the only reward the company has built into their system is one of promotion to supervisor. It's the only reward that comes with a pay increase, increased benefits, and increased responsibility. Now we're finding that we must create a multi-track approach. We've got to recognize people who are not looking to become supervisors but certainly should be rewarded for the progress they make. For those who prefer to become managers and supervisors, in addition to formal training, a track must be provided that will include mentoring and coaching as they take on new roles and responsibilities.

Wright

Sam, there are about as many definitions of success as there are people I've asked to define it but I'm going to give it another shot. What would be your definition?

Slay

I don't think my definition is much different than many others' except in order—the travel, destination, and ultimate attainment of a life that you want individually. You've noticed that folks talk a lot about wealth and being rich and it's simply methods and assets used to attain what we desire to do, have, and be which doesn't necessarily involve money. In fact, quite frequently it doesn't involve money at all.

Wright

I have a good friend who loves to say, "I don't want to be a millionaire—I just want to live like one." Why do you think some people fail while others are successful?

Slay

In my case I think determination, creativity, and a lot of family support contributed to my success. I think that a lot of it has to do with being willing to do what others are not. For example, a successful athlete trains harder, more intensely, and never lets anything get in his/her way. It's that same way with anything—you can't let roadblocks deter you. Everyone will encounter roadblocks they must overcome.

Wright

In other words, you can have momentary failure in some of the tasks you're doing but you don't have to accept failure as the final goal.

Slay

Exactly; and you *will* fail. If someone tells you that you can't fail or you've become a failure, that's not true. It's the failures that make you stronger and show you the right way to accomplish whatever it is you're trying to accomplish.

Wright

You talk about being a leader, a coach, and a consultant. What does this represent?

Slay

I don't think anyone should consider starting out in a leadership role. First you have to follow; not only do you have to follow but you have to be a good follower. Then you can be a coach so others will lead and then you can become a consultant to share the knowledge you gain from leading and coaching.

Wright

Back in the '70s I was in a leadership conference in Waco, Texas. A brilliant man there told me, "David, if you envision yourself as a great leader and you look around and no one's following, you're only out for a walk." I've heard about statistics that indicate two percent of the nation is made up of leaders and ninety-eight percent are followers. That sounds bad but the people in the ninety-eight percent really *want* to follow. To be a leader you almost have to choose to be one, right?

Slay

It's easier to follow. Obviously it's more rewarding to lead from time to time but it's a learned behavior, it's not for everybody, and not everyone wants to do it. There are others who don't want to follow constantly, they want to be out in the front, and they want to be a leader. We all must be capable of reverting back from a leadership role to a follower's role. A brief example would be taking on a new assignment we are not prepared for—for example, taking on a supervisory role we're not prepared for. In that case we have to count on someone else to basically lead the way.

Wright

I guarantee you I lead in my company but I follow at home. Why doesn't everyone learn to lead?

Slay

On average, people are looking for leadership and to be led. You're taking on quite a responsibility when you want to be the leader. If anything fails, you're the failure—not the followers—because you're the one out in front, you're the one who is pushing and/or pulling these people in a certain direction. It's like public speaking—not everyone wants to get up there and take a chance on making a fool out of themselves; but you need to be the fool from time to time to see where you are going.

Wright

When I look at the ultimate leadership role of the presidency of the United States, it comes with some real serious downsides. About fifty percent of the country doesn't like what he's doing. Consider also, how many presidents get shot at.

Slay

It can be a thankless position. "We want you to do this and if you don't do it the way we *all* want it done you're in trouble."

Wright

As a speaker, trainer, coach, and consultant, what makes your philosophy different?

Slay

I would say I use a different approach. I'm convinced there is room for many more promoters of this philosophy. It's like comedians—no one would argue that there's enough laughter in the world so there's always room for more comedians. I will admit I view things a bit differently and I enjoy viewing things differently. It's also fun to look at it from different perspectives. Sometimes our background tends to give us tunnel vision. New eyes never prevented anyone from seeing, so you've got to look at it from a different view or angle. If you don't feel like you have a different perspective, you've got to seek out that perspective.

If you've been a supervisor for a long period of time you tend to think about things only from an administrative standpoint. Maybe you should consider things from a line position.

Wright

Do you stay fairly positive most of the time?

Slay

Yes, I do. It's a whole lot more fun. There are so many things to drag you down if you don't stay positive. Of course, everybody's an optimist in a positive world but you should always try to be an optimist when things are *not* going your way—that's the true test of the optimist.

Wright

The reason I asked the question is that I've had friends who have been in police work. You have been chief of police and may relate to this. My friends seem to look at the darker side of things because of their experiences—they see so much bad going on. How have you been able to stay positive when you've got all that in your background?

Slay

The only way you can do that, especially for over twenty-four years, is to filter things into your mind that are positive. You've got to read, research, and you've got to focus on the positive as much as possible because you've got to flush the negative. If you have a negative conversation, people tend to jump right in, but if you have a positive conversation, people feel good about it, it's just not as entertaining. If you don't look beyond the current job responsibilities—especially in law enforcement—you can easily get caught up in negativity.

When I was in law enforcement one of the things we learned in community policing was that the majority of people are good people. Our job just required us to deal with the bad people the majority of the time.

Wright

You have been successful bringing the private sector perspective to a government bureaucratic environment. Would you tell our readers how you accomplished this?

Slay

The government survives by public cooperation and the private sector business survives by cash. If they don't do a better job, they're out of business. Unfortunately, the government doesn't see it that way. They survive by tax dollars, while complacent to believe this won't change. When you look at the operation, you only have to look around at some of the private companies that are successful such as fast food restaurants and other service industries and ask who is doing it better. We don't get a financial return, from a government perspective, but we get a cooperative return and we are required to stretch government dollars further.

If you look at the way the government has always operated (I'm sure you've heard these kinds of stories such as the $200 hammer), we get so bogged down in paperwork and the traditional approach, we "can't see the proverbial forest for the trees." The way the government manages budgets is totally counterproductive. We encourage people to frivolously use money at the end of a budget cycle when we should be encouraging them to hold on to that money for a later and better purchase and add it to the next year's budget. In the private sector, it's only on paper anyway—that money exists—so you're going to add it into your next year's productivity spending.

You have to look at the successful side of the private sector and re-invent that philosophy in government.

Wright

I read a lot in today's news about private companies taking over the operation of prisons, for example. They take an old way of doing things and put their new perspective on it. The ones I read about seem to be proving every day that this is a better way to do it. I'm not sure that's true.

Slay

We have that situation where I live. There's a private firm that handles the jail facility; they also handle some nearby prison facilities. I think the good thing is they're looking at the bottom line much harder than the government side would and the government figures if it can't control its budget, it will simply raise taxes. The private sector doesn't have a taxing capability; they've either got to make the service better, cut costs where they can, and then make money on the other side or it's bankrupt.

Another thing we find is sometimes in government we're mistaken to think that the public will not pay for what they want. If they want something such as a private security force, or they want their own police department, or whatever, they'll get it. You'll find that police departments have been taken over by subdivisions or homeowners' associations and those personnel are making pretty good salaries. There's a reason and it's because the community demands a greater or particular level of service and they're willing to pay for it.

I'm glad you're bringing this up because another point is the fact that often, in government, we think our job is secure because we work for the government. Now, in the twenty-first century, we're seeing those jobs being removed either because of technology advancements or replacement by the private sector organizations that do it better, cheaper, and they make a handsome profit.

Wright

What is one of the first things you recommend we do in any business?

Slay

Try to change the way we do business on a day-to-day basis. In business today we've got a challenge to prioritize what's most important. In my opinion, people are the most important component in any organization. They are the common denominator in every organization. We think of customers as being number one but it's a proven fact that if you make the employee number one, the customer will benefit.

Another thing we should do is look at our systems. Statistics reveal eighty-five percent of the problems in an organization evolve around systems. Only fifteen percent involve human error.

With that in mind, we have to look at our systems to see what causes a breakdown or a disruption and secondly we need to make sure that our employees are internally motivated to perform.

Wright

Sam, I know the title of this book is *Masters of Success* and I think everything our authors think and their combined experiences go into their being successful. I want to get off the business topic for a moment, though, and ask you a question. I know that you believe family violence is a national epidemic. Will you speak to that? Is there anything we can do about it? How bad is it?

Slay

Dr. Peter Sylvester, director of the Bay County Health Department, told me that in his opinion he believed there are three different epidemics in the nation today. These are not in any particular order but he said one of the epidemics is HIV/AIDS, another is obesity, and another is domestic violence.

One of the problems that I see is the "blind-eye syndrome"—the public turning a blind eye to family violence and the thought that it still remains a family matter. It is an international as well as a national concern. Police departments can't be held accountable for what they don't know, but they certainly must be held accountable for what is reported to them, what they respond to, and what they investigate. We've got to do a better job. The job is not being done.

There are several first responders to domestic violence. They are:

- The general public—individuals who first witness or who are told about a violent situation,
- Law enforcement,
- State attorneys or district attorneys (depending on your region of the country), and
- Judges.

Overall we don't do a very good job there. We have the tools—most states and the federal government have placed tremendous laws on the books to be utilized as tools to protect victims of domestic violence.

The next problem I see is the philosophy of understanding the dynamics of a domestic violence situation. Beyond that, if we can accomplish better response with first responders and create a greater understanding of what's really going on in the family unit, then and only then can we effectively combat domestic violence.

We tend to think stranger-on-stranger violence is more terrible and family violence is not nearly as bad. Yet we are a country greatly impacted financially, emotionally, and certainly morally by what's going on in family violence.

Wright

As a citizen, it's always amazed me when either the man or woman has caused harm to their spouse, the police are called to determine who's at fault, and then the spouse drops charges. Is there any way that the government (i.e., the county or the city) could prosecute?

Slay

You hit it on the head—that's a very good question. That's exactly what is supposed to happen. Law enforcement is supposed to remove the victim as far as necessary from the prosecution. Now, does this mean that if you have a cooperative victim, they shouldn't be on the witness stand telling the story? No, that's not at all what I'm saying. More likely than not, through threat, fear, intimidation, or maybe even love for that spouse, they go to court and represent the other party or they try to have the charges dropped. We have the laws on the books, we have the appropriate philosophy, it's just not being dealt with properly by first responders.

The minute a domestic violence incident occurs, we should gather all of the evidence we can (because that's as much evidence as we're likely to get) and then we should prosecute to the fullest extent of the law without the victim being able to interrupt that process. The example I use is that of a homicide victim. The victim is certainly not able to come to court and testify and so they are excluded from the process because they're deceased. In the domestic violence situation, we should prosecute and we should do this based on the evidence.

You're exactly right when you indicate we shouldn't allow a victim who can't understand the emotional roller coaster interfere with the process. As an instructor I am able to explain what's going on in this environment and why victims don't want to prosecute. But until people understand, they will continue to think that if a victim wants to, they should be allowed to drop charges. This is not like the theft of a piece of property like a John Deere tractor, this is different—it involves an emotional bond and connection between the victim and the offender. When people don't understand this, I ask them, "How many of you here in the room have made a bad decision based on emotion?" Of course, they all raise their hands. Then I tell them, "Well, there you are." We've done things that we would look at now from a logical and objective standpoint later and think, "I would never do that." Yes you would—under the right circumstances you would do the very same thing.

Wright

Getting back to the subject of business, I do have a final business question for you. How does "total customer focus" create business success?

Slay

It's ultimately the customer who puts money in our pockets. Every customer is waiting for the next big thing. Every time a new restaurant or store opens they flock to try it out. Maybe it's good and maybe it's *very* good but they're always waiting for the next big thing.

Recently I read the book *Raving Fans*. I thought the authors, Ken Blanchard and Sheldon Bowles, put it in real perspective: satisfied customers are no longer enough. You have to get customers raving about your product or service so that when the next big thing comes along they won't permanently leave you. That's a tall order but it's worth capturing.

Wright

I'll bet you've led an interesting life in government service, sales, and marketing. I really appreciate your taking this time to discuss success and success in business.

Slay

Thank you David, I enjoyed it.

Wright

Today we've been talking with Sam Slay who is a retired chief of police. He's worked in field operations and later, vice president of sales and marketing for a wireless Internet company. Sam is now a speaker, coach, and consultant. He is President of the Bay County Domestic Violence Task Force and he believes, as we have found, that family violence is a national epidemic. Right now he is the owner of Sam Slay & Associates, a speaking, coaching, and consulting business and 357 Solutions, LLC, an employee and organizational development company. He can be contacted at Sam@SamSlay.com, Sam@357Solutions.com, or by phone at (850) 596-7335.

Sam, thank you so much for being with us today on *Masters of Success*.

Slay

Thank you, it was a pleasure.

About The Author

Sam Slay brings twenty-four years of government experience. He has owned and operated several businesses. He is a retired Chief of Police. He has worked as Chief of Field Operations and later as vice president of sales and marketing for a wireless internet company. His opportunity to manage personnel has been most challenging and rewarding. He recognizes the "Power of People" and the "Power of Enthusiasm." Sam is a speaker, coach, and consultant. He has focused on supervisory skills, working with staff to promote productivity and a positive work environment. His goal is to create a greater "Return On Investment" (ROI) from staff. Sam is the President of the Bay County Domestic Violence Task Force. He believes "Family Violence" is a national epidemic. Sam is also owner of Sam Slay & Associates, a company providing speaking, coaching, and consulting services. He is president and CEO of 357 Solutions, LLC, providing employee and organizational training and development.

Sam Slay

Sam Slay & Associates

357 Solutions, LLC

P.O. Box 1308

Panama City, Florida 32402-1308

Phone: 850.596.7335

www.SamSlay.com

www.357Solutions.com

Chapter Six

DONNA HICKEY

THE INTERVIEW

David E. Wright (Wright)

Donna Hickey is one of the brightest voices promoting self-esteem and motivational seminars. Her presentations articulate and endorse intensive personal and professional development. With her powerful inspirational style she challenges her audiences, leaving them asking for more. She has traveled many continents conducting seminars and workshops while speaking in a variety of fields including housing, hospitality, airline, financial, communication, women's groups, human resource organizations, and the education system.

As a recognized speaker, Donna's focus is sales, customer service, and people skills seminars, and workshops. Her clients say, "What sets her apart is her wacky sense of humor along with her honest, straight-to-the-point opinions."

She's been quoted by the *Chicago Tribune* as well as industry focused publications that specialize in sales, customer service, and developing people skills as well as in newsletters regarding the apartment industry and sales management among others.

In addition to receiving many awards of accomplishment and recognition from the companies Donna has worked for, she has been recognized as a professional entrepreneur in *Who's Who Magazine*.

She's an active member of the National Speakers Association, a board member for the Illinois National Speakers Association, and ASTD (American Society of Training and Development). Donna is also on the Curriculum Development Committee for the National Apartment Association. After twenty years of part-time schooling Donna finally received her degree from Canterbury University.

Donna's seminars offer a serious, fun, and creative learning process.

Donna, welcome to *Masters of Success*.

Donna Hickey (Hickey)

I am honored that you and your company sought me out as one of the new *Masters of Success* in the twenty-first century. When I learned of this fabulous project and that you wanted me to be part of it, I could not have been more honored. In fact, most of the information disclosed in this chapter has never been published. My very private struggles, my climb out of despair, and my road to recovery are all part of my success. I hope readers are moved and inspired by my story.

Wright

So what was your motivation to becoming an entrepreneur?

Hickey

What a complex question. In order to answer that question, I think we should delve into past history first and then get straight to the point.

When I started in the multi-family housing industry, it wasn't something that I went to high school for and said, "Gee, I can't wait to graduate high school to become a leasing consultant." No, that happened quite by accident.

Let me explain...

When I was young, growing up and high school age, you could say I, along with the rest of my family, had issues. Having said that, while still in high school I moved out of my house and then graduated a half year early. At that time in my life I had to be in the retail industry. I had a dream of one day becoming a fashion designer but, oops! Someone forgot to tell me I needed a college degree for that.

My fiancé and I needed an apartment. We needed steady work—steady income—and a roof over our heads. So one day, back in 1980 when I went into the rental office to pay the rent, there stood the sign all gleaming with hope: "Rental Agent Wanted." As I heard the chimes going off in my head, I immediately asked to fill out an application and that was the beginning of my illustrious twenty-five-year-long career in property management.

It's amazing how the way you think about yourself changes the way you think about the world. I learned that the only way to change the world is to change myself and that journey began for me when I turned twenty-five years old.

Having come from a poor family (with benefits—my mom worked for the airline industry and we flew for free), a single parent household, we were more like rogue dogs who ran around willy-nilly in the neighborhood. We were a family with issues.

At the age of twenty-five years old I admitted myself into an alcohol/drug treatment center, not only to battle those demons but to also conquer an out-of-control eating disorder. A year later I walked out of Hazelton a changed person. The lessons I learned would be tested and learned again during the next twenty years. Failure and the introspection that failure caused me has led me to the extraordinary levels of abundance I am currently experiencing.

It also began a twenty-year journey of research and study in the areas of self-discovery, self-development, human potential, and how to shatter the self-limiting beliefs that hold us back. The question that always comes up is how can we tap into the power of our subconscious mind to achieve abundance? How am I going to achieve abundance, in all areas of my life: relationships, health, finance, sexuality, and overall success?

While on my journey, one simple insight that kept replaying itself was how I was pre-programmed from childhood. As young toddlers all of us have experienced limiting and/or lack of beliefs that have continued right into adulthood. We are assaulted with negative messages twenty-four hours a day, seven days a week, not only by television, but also at the workplace from family, friends, the Internet and finally, the news media. If you are hearing all these messages, they are entering your subconscious mind.

Until you uncover and counteract this programming, it exists on a subconscious level, causing you to sabotage the personal and professional success you are seeking. This subconscious programming also infects the way you feel about work, relationships, money, sex, and your body. It affects whether you get sick and how fast you heal when you become ill.

I also discovered that ninety percent of reaching any achievement is the belief that you will do so. A change in your thinking and belief systems can nurture new, healthy confidence. Your new confidence causes you to act differently and that can put you over the top.

Discoveries like these and many more like them, led me to the work I do today. I believe I have truly discovered my life's assignment. Sharing what I have learned about the power of the mind and the principals of abundance has opened new opportunities around the world for me.

This life experience is what brought me to becoming an entrepreneur. I believe that we need to give back; that is the gift—the gift of knowledge.

Wright

Wow! Donna, that's quite a story! So, being a wife, are you a mother as well?

Hickey

It's not often that you can find someone you want to spend the rest of your life with and who isn't going to run when the going gets tough. My husband, Roger, and I have been together for twenty years. We met doing some charity work together raising money for a state run organization.

Since Roger has two daughters I had decided when I was very young I didn't want children. I felt I had babysat my entire youth away and selfishly I wanted to live my adulthood and grow up myself.

Wright

So what challenges have you faced balancing business and your personal life?

Hickey

Since Roger has retired we have the opportunity for him to manage the company, me, and the house. I feel compelled to dedicate this chapter to my husband Roger. Without his support, unselfishness, and strength, and above all else his patience, I could not do what I am doing. Who else would encourage his wife to globe-trot around the world speaking, presenting, conducting workshops, and coaching? I am gone for weeks at a time. I am blessed to have such a great guy.

Wright

You know, I've made this statement to a lot of our other authors: A man told me one time that if you're walking down the road and you see a turtle sitting on top of a fencepost you can bet that he didn't get up there by himself. So who have your mentors been—those people who have impacted your life and your success?

Hickey

Mentors? I've had none; it's a bit of a sad story. When I was a young girl growing up, I was always searching for a mentor to look up to—someone to teach me who I am and what I am supposed to do with this thing called life and all the amenities that come with it.

I think that when I went into treatment, I leaned on that program; that is why there was a twenty-year-long journey of self-discovery.

When I met Roger, I had no idea what to do with this guy. Remember, I was this "wild dog" out there living like a stray doing what I had to do to survive. That's the gift my parents gave me—the will to survive. I thank Joe McDonald, my marriage coach, for his guidance and mentorship. At least he helped me in the success of my marriage so far.

From a work standpoint, my parents had great work ethic. That's where they were all the time. We didn't grow up in the '60s and '70s with a June Cleaver and a *"Leave it to Beaver"* kind of life. My dad owned his own company and thus we learned to work at a young age. I went to the Wheeling, Illinois, Jaycees Babysitting Clinic when I was eleven years old. I knew that if I could get the certificate, I could baby-sit and make money, so I did. I haven't stopped working since.

In my career in the multi-housing industry, I have great friends and acquaintances, but one person stands out amongst the many— Tom Custer. I worked for and with Tom for eight years and each year I learned more about working environments and people skills than most people might learn in a lifetime. Tom accelerated that experience for me and I will always be grateful.

Someone who touched my life for a short period of time (I wish it had been longer) is John Gray. I'll always remember his people management style—the way he talked to people and brought out the very best. He too is a great mentor.

When I started my company "Donna L. Hickey Presents..." a Back to Basics Company, I did it on my own. I woke up when I was forty years old and thought, "There has to be more to life than this." I have stumbled and bumbled all the way. I never sat down and wrote a business plan. Back to Basics Training and Consulting Company was a slow developing process, so I thought. I rushed headlong into building, developing, and rolling out one thing after another. In the beginning, I did ask colleagues for help. I have to admit, I am the one in a million who has had more roadblocks than anyone I know. People will say to me today, "If you need help, all you have to do is ask, reach out, and seek." However, my experience was/is people will only put their faith and trust in you *after* you have proven yourself, *not before*.

Please don't get me wrong. I am not feeling sorry for myself. What I did was become stronger because of all the obstacles. My focus has changed directions a million times. I've spent more money than anyone I know. I could write a book on all things *not* to do. Now, after four years of owning these companies, they are on solid ground and moving successfully forward.

The folks who have really helped lately would be the National Speakers Association. It's a great place to start if you are ever thinking about getting into the speaking business.

Because of this experience, I designed a program called "Managing Upwards and Mentoring Below." It's designed to explore the many avenues we take on this road called life and to uncover who in the organization can help you in those challenging situations and mentor you on an on-going basis. There are certain qualities that you are looking for including a mutual respect. Now, mentoring may be well established in the male work place. I found, however, through research and interviews that this is not necessarily true in the female work place. Mentoring happens at all levels of professionalism, not just at the executive level.

That was a long answer to a simple question David; but thanks for asking it.

Wright

So what is the most important piece of advice you would give to a twenty-year-old version of yourself or perhaps someone just starting out?

Hickey

When starting a company you want to reduce your amount of stress as much as possible. You want to be able to think about processes not problems. It's the same thing I talk about when I am conducting a training seminar—focus on principals not personalities, that way you keep your goal in mind.

I found out about Service Corps of Retired Executives (S.C.O.R.E.), and had I known that small business training network was available then, I would have sought out a retired professional to assist me in the development of my companies and to coach my mind regarding my new venture.

I became so good at networking and finding resources that I have a book coming out in 2006 called *Donna Hickey Presents—The 7 Secrets to Successful Networking.* I now sit with young entrepreneurs and help them map or chart a course in business development.

When it comes to money, I wish I had obtained a business loan—maybe a small business loan. Instead, I used charge cards to start my company. When I went to the banks to see if I could flip this over to a business loan, I was turned down and had to find other alternative options. I would not recommend this. If you need capital in the beginning, get it. It was so hard when I started.

I read the following quote recently and thought how true it is, "In the early stages of anything new, management, coworkers, family, and friends can't be bothered, since they are skeptical. They never really like things that haven't been done before. That's why Christopher Columbus had so much trouble getting financing"—*Ivan Seidenberg, Chairman and CEO of Verizon.*

My recommendation is to focus on the building of the company not on the money you'll make.

Wright

Absolutely. I remember when I started out in business for myself in '69. I went to the bank and tried to borrow $2,500.00 to start this business and they turned me down; but I did it anyway. I borrowed money from a friend and paid it back at about 2000 percent interest. I remember that the same guy who turned me down at the bank loaned me $40,000 on my signature five years later to buy a computer!

You know, sometimes it is hard to get help. Most of the people I ask about mentors tell me all these wonderful stories and I'm thinking, you know, my story is more like yours. I had very little help and almost no training.

That's why I think the most important training in the world is the training that you do for yourself. I used to use my own money to go to seminars and workshops and buy books.

Hickey

I can't agree with you more in regards to training, seminars, books on tape, and so on. I have always been a champion for education. All I ever wanted was a college degree. I believe that if a person works hard enough and sets aside all those pre-programmed childhood subconscious messages, that person can attain anything his or her heart and mind desires to accomplish. It takes hard work though. I am a student for life. I continue to attend training, education, and speaking events. One is never too smart to stop learning.

Because of my passion for education, both companies, Donna Hickey Presents... and Back to Basics Training and Consulting Company, has introduced this summer, "The Leasing Notebook"™ for the multi-housing industry and then this book *Masters of Success* in early 2006. Also in early 2006 we will be releasing *Donna Hickey Presents— the 7 Secrets to Successful Networking* and the long awaited *Trench Warfare—25 years as a Foot Soldier in Property Management.*" In 2006 we are also releasing "Leasing Power Live."™ These are monthly CDs that contain information from soup to nuts about the apartment industry. We will interview several professionals for each CD and each month the subscriber will receive a CD containing different challenges. This way we are hearing from real life professionals on "how to" situations.

The proudest session that I want to brag about is, "Live Your Abundant Life, Stop Moving Forward with The Brakes On." Not only is this a stand-alone session, it's a workshop, a seminar, and a how-to monthly training program. We are very excited about this program rolling out in 2006.

All of my seminars are serious and yet fun. We pick real life struggles and put them into challenging seminars to stimulate thinking and change. I am not a feel good presenter with fluff and stuff. We have deep conversations with humor and fun, meaningful content, and measurable successes. Then we feel good about the accomplishments. Education is fun and meaningful—I deliver just that.

Wright

What has been your greatest challenge in your entrepreneurial career?

Hickey

I always think my biggest challenge is getting in front of the decision maker and proving that I can perform—the consulting work that

I do, the speaking, and the "Return On Investment" with the training sessions I perform. I have been regarded as one of the best in the industry, and yet talk is cheap—you really have to earn your stripes and pay your dues. Even though I think that statement is ridiculous, it's true. Breaking through barriers and misconceptions is tough. My friend John Gray said it best when he said, "The cream always rises to the top. Have patience and you'll get there." He couldn't be more right.

It's hard to promote yourself. I remember when I first started speaking and training, people would ask me all the time what was my "niche"—what was my expertise? I would reply, "Sales, customer service, and people skills." Then they wanted me to boil it down again from there. Even though I didn't want to be pigeonholed, people will do it for you whether you like it or not.

I spoke with a friend of mine who had hired me for a marketing session the previous year. When I found out her association had a state function, I asked if I could submit a presentation. She said, "It's not marketing, are you sure you have something to add?" This confirmed to me that I was not communicating all that I have to offer. Since then I've changed my marketing. I thought this was interesting because you really have to be careful about what you put out there, and/or what you don't put out there.

The bottom line is, people need to get to know you—really know you—where you came from, who you are, and where you are going. I focused so much on the building of Donna Hickey Presents... that I forgot people needed to know who I really am.

Wright

I remember going into business many, many years ago. The question I had for myself was, who motivates the motivator? So my question for you is, what inspires you to maintain your enthusiasm during challenging times?

Hickey

Believe me, my husband went on a motorcycle trip during the summer and I teared up for two weeks straight, not because he was gone (I'm glad he got out of the house and had some fun), but because I needed time to myself, reflection, renewal, and I needed peace.

I had been running for years. I finally had a chance to stop and think and all the work details and problems came rushing in headlong: the start-up capital, the continuation of always looking for business, the endless hours writing books, articles, programs, and consulting projects—it all hit me at once. What am I doing? It was the best two weeks I could have dreamed of.

My sister Julie also owns her own company. I called her and babbled on for a few minutes until she reminded me of her business loan and mortgage. I did feel better knowing she had a bigger risk than I had. She was a treasure and let me babble on. Once I was done, we put our heads together for brainstorming and direction modifications. We eliminated a division of my company—I had a recruiting company and a temp agency that I could not devote the time to—so we jettisoned that division. I came away focused and recharged.

On a day-to-day basis, the feedback, the success stories, the e-mails, and the phone calls keep me going. There isn't a day that goes by that I haven't been involved in a conversation about the gifts I gave during a session, seminar, or workshop, or simply an article someone read.

This past year I rolled out a new seminar called, "Good People Don't Quit Good Companies, They Quit Toxic Bosses." I have been hired all over the world to give this seminar: here in the USA, Europe Asia, and the Middle East to name a few. People laugh at the title and then say, "Boy that's the truth." When participants attend this session they walk away with a toolbox full of ideas, tools, and truths they can put into place in their life—a simple idea or change to make their world better. When that happens, change occurs in every aspect of their life. They are grateful for the peace. I am always grateful and honored by those folks. They keep me motivated.

Wright

Shakespeare had a good idea, "kill all the lawyers," so we can kill all the bosses. Wait a minute, *I'm* a boss—can't do that!

Hickey

Too funny! But I think that's the enthusiasm. I think you know you love what you do. People ask me all the time, "Oh my God! You're self-employed—you have all these businesses! How do you keep going?" I just think—and you probably feel the same way—if it's something you truly believe in and the passion is in your heart, it's not work.

Wright

So how do you measure success?

Hickey

Joel Osteen, pastor of the world wide Christian outreach center, Lakewood Church in Texas, said it best when he said it's a change in thinking. If you get up in the morning and dread going to work, hate the drive, hate the people you work with, hate doing the dishes when you come home, and hate having to go to bed just to do it all over again the next day, something has to change. Be grateful you have that day in the first place.

I have had an incredible journey so far in my life. I got to spend twenty years figuring out who Donna Hickey is. Most people won't get a chance to do that until their kids are older and then *they* are older. My life today is abundant in many ways. I have a sense of peace in my soul. I love to give back, I volunteer all over the place. I came from such a horrible place in life (lost, drinking, drugging, eating, no sense of peace) that I am very grateful for what I have today—and each day. This to me is my measurement of success. I've not slid backwards, I am living my abundant life and the brakes are off, meaning I'm not just existing, I'm living—I'm alive.

When it comes to business, success is standing the test of time, pushing through barriers, taking risks, knowing and believing in who I am and that what I have to offer will benefit others. Most importantly, it's having repeat business clients.

Good mental, physical, and emotional health and being able to pay the bills are also measurements for success.

Wright

Is success measurable or is it just a state of mind?

Hickey

The philosophical part of me says it's a state of mind. I think it's both—in my world it has to be both. You have to be able to measure it and you have to know that success is a state of mind. I believe people are driven by the engine in their brain. If people don't believe in success, if they don't believe that they deserve success, and if they can't break through the barrier of fear, it will be very difficult for them to succeed.

Wright

I remember a brilliant man telling me something many, many years ago when we were worried about all kinds of diseases including

HIV, cancers, and diabetes. He told me that the most prominent disease in the twenty-first century is low self-esteem.

Hickey

Oh, absolutely.

"Live your Abundant Life, Stop Moving Forward with the Brakes On," talks about just that. "Low Self Esteem," addresses the barriers it creates, the lack of confidence it creates, and the poison that pollutes your mind. I suffered from it, overcame it, and now I teach others to get beyond it.

Childhood programming has a lot to do with this topic including "fear." I read a book when I was fired from my very first job titled, *Feel the Fear and Do it Anyway*. It changed my life. I have tested that book and its theories beyond what is normal.

I am your typical kid who went to school, I had a lazy eye (so I looked funny), and I had buckteeth. I had all sorts of learning disabilities. As I grew and went on to high school, I was shy—I was the person who had the lowest self-esteem on the planet—so much so that I would tell my teachers, my college professors, and classmates, "Don't ever have me do an oral presentation in class. If that is a requirement, please flunk me now." I remember having such low self-esteem I didn't even want to take driver's education. I was scared to death to drive or make a decision for myself. Ha! *That* changed!

To get beyond low self-esteem there are stages you have to go through and it takes time to learn to take risks, challenge the limits you set for yourself, and work harder to be a better person. I know—I did it. I was also in the Parkside system as a volunteer for ten years helping teens overcome this very issue too. Today I speak in the education system on drugs and alcohol prevention. I lost a sister at the age of thirty-four to drug and alcohol abuse.

Wright

So how has your mission changed since you began?

Hickey

When I first started "Back to Basics, Training the ABCs of Property Management," I was thinking small (i.e., consulting, recruiting, temping, etc.). But business began to spin and all sorts of opportunities began to pop up. The more I spoke with people the more I kept learning about other opportunities. I attended every convention I could. I attended seminars because there were people I wanted to hear. I spoke for free my first year so I could learn the business; I even spent my own money on travel and transport. The more I did that, the more I learned.

When I heard of the National Speakers Association (NSA), I went to my first meeting in September 2004. That is when my business changed. For the first time in my life I was with like-minded people: gracious, professional, and willing to help—a true gift. I learned to build a better business framework. I learned there were people who wanted to help me and I learned that these people were kind, helpful, and had strong ethics. They changed the way I do business.

For the very first year, I attended every meeting, here in the U.S. and abroad. I met as many people as I could, asked questions, and sought guidance. I will always be grateful to NSA—USA and NSA, Illinois. I attended the International Summit in Singapore and rolled out my seminar "Good People Don't Quit Good Companies, They Quit Toxic Bosses." I met so many great people that I have been invited back to speak on this topic in Manila at an HR convention, including conventions in Singapore and Hong Kong. I always knew my business would be international; I just never thought it would happen this soon.

Now I speak internationally, nationally, and regionally. I started Donna Hickey Presents... for corporate America and the education system. My Web site is www.donnahickey.com. Back to Basics, Training the ABC's of Property Management is for the housing industry and the site for that is: www.basicsabc.com.

Wright

I've been booking speakers for sixteen years now. I love great titles. That "Toxic Boss" title you have is a great title. I love that.

I guess my favorite of all time is when I went to a red carpet, real estate franchise meeting in Las Vegas back in somewhere around '82 or '83. I arrived at the hotel and they gave us the package for the next day's meetings. The keynoter's address was titled, "You Can't Lead a Charge Up the Hill if You Think You Look Funny Sitting on a Horse." I thought, "I am there and I've got to hear what this guy has to say."

With all the hard work and dedication and everything you put up with all through the years—teaching yourself—and all those things that are so difficult, is your reward financial, emotional, or is it both?

Hickey

Everybody likes to know that they have the freedom to make as little or as much money as they want. I think it's about the opportunities that present themselves. We live in our little safe cocoons because we don't like change. There's a sense of fear that belongs to that—the fear of the unknown—not knowing what's on the other side of that, and I thrive on change. I like upsetting the apple cart and seeing what happens. There aren't many people who like to do that.

I think there's a psychological benefit in knowing that you're giving away something. There are other people out there who come from dysfunctional families. There are other people out there who haven't had the structured life that involved college and all of the safety that a good home life provides. I think it's a lot about knowing you can succeed without all the mental garbage. Perhaps you come from a poor family, who tells you that you can't make it; or you come from an ethnic background and people say, "Well, if you make it you'll be one in a million." You can make it in the life conditions where you are. We have these barriers—these boundaries—and it's about breaking through all of that and saying, "Hey, I have something to say/do/see/experience—with all of this adversity I've made it!"

I think for me it's a couple of things. Entrepreneurship gives me the platform to go out and to develop, to assist, and guide. Then financially it gives me the freedom to make as much or as little as I want. I think from a psychological standpoint it's giving back. "Living a prosperous life is our right. So go out and seek out your abundance," so says Catherine Ponder.

Wright

Absolutely. For me, learning is so important. I turn a back flip every time I learn something new—I just love to learn. Do you think that you would have learned as much as you know now had you not been an entrepreneur?

Hickey

No.

Wright

It's sad, really. When you work for corporations and don't learn it's really sad. I worked for so many corporations for so many years and as I look back on it, almost all of my learning was done on my own. It's really sad.

Hickey

I agree with that whole-heartedly. I work with a client out on the East Coast; this company has been running for over fifty years. It's a multi-tiered, multi-generation company. Some of the folks are my age. One of them, who has been mentored by his father, got stuck in this old world way of thinking while one of the other gentlemen I spoke with came from corporate America, worked on Wall Street, knows the game, and thinks very progressively. Having worked with them on a consultant basis for awhile I have been able to see that the gentleman who worked on Wall Street is being pulled into this traditional mindset. I'm thinking, "Don't go that way! We already have five people in the organization who are thinking that way; you were the only breath of fresh air!"

When it comes to learning, it's taking a look at *all* of the learning processes that are out there rather than just looking at it from a narrow focus. That has been one of the biggest rewards from entrepreneurship—looking at the world from such a global perspective.

So many people never make it out of their own neighborhoods, let alone out of their own states. We grew up poor but we had benefits. As I said earlier, my mom has always worked for the airline industry. She worked for Fin Air, Trans Air Portugal, Kuwait Airways, and EL AL (which is Air Israel) and now works for Singapore Airlines. My entire life has been exposed to this global traveling. I had a sister who lived in England, and I had a brother who lived in Florence, Manila, Taiwan, and Bahrain.

What would happen around the holidays is that we would have all these people from around the world join us. The conversation would be global in perspective and entertaining. I was able to interact with many different people in my life when I was a youngster. I was exposed to many things, yet I was learning and thinking big. The unique thing about experiencing so many differences is that, rather than having preconceived ideas as a result of media hype and someone else's opinion, my sisters, my brother, and I were able to make up our own minds on different belief systems and understand their impact globally at a young age.

My family had always been exposed to the element of travel—this kind of busy lifestyle—and I think it gives a different perspective on really what's out there. One becomes really broad in one's thinking—very big in scope.

So you asked me earlier what impact this has on my marriage and how it impacts my home life. My husband lived in Germany for five and one-half years because he was in the Air Force during the Vietnam War. So again, he was very well traveled. Having traveled so much he has so much more to talk about and can see the impact education has on people. He can see the differences in the American employee versus the Asian employee or the European employee and the impact their company has on them or doesn't have on them. It's very eye-opening.

Wright

No wonder you're an entrepreneur and no wonder you go around teaching people. What a great life you must have.

Hickey

Thank you. I have been blessed. People ask me all the time, how I can possibly be married, operate two companies, and have a life. I existed from age one until twenty-five, then, from twenty-five to forty I learned who I was. I traveled, I learned how to ride a motorcycle, and travel cross country on it, I took flying lessons, I owned and rode horses, I studied the American Indian in college for four years, visited an Indiana reservation, flew over the Badlands in helicopters, owned a boat out on Lake Michigan, and learned to love.

Now I work at a passion I love and it doesn't seem like work. When I started Back to Basics, I worked 27/7 for three solid years— no vacation, no family get-togethers, and no parties of my own. I tell interested people that I am sure when Oprah Winfrey works, she's not thinking about the next family vacation. When Donald Trump is home, I am sure he's working, thinking, building, and outlining deals. Your mind keeps going, you are exploring, you feel compelled, there is no vacation and free thinking time, it's a love, a passion, and a destiny.

Wright

Donna Hickey, what an interesting conversation.

Hickey

Thanks to Insight Publishing for inviting me to be part of this wonderful project. I am honored to be chosen among my esteemed colleagues to be part of this exciting opportunity. This chapter has reveled a part of my life that had been separated from the whole for a long time. Not only am I grateful for the opportunity to share my life's struggles but to also to recount the journey, the joy, and the success. I hope I have given someone the gift of knowledge, the strength, or the will so that others too can strike out on their own, take a risk, find a mentor, and succeed. Thanks David, it's been a pleasure for me too.

Wright

Donna, after interviewing you and hearing your story I can see why everything you touch turns to gold—you are fortunate to be living such an abundant and prosperous life.

I understand now why your seminars and workshops are so popular and in high demand.

I look forward to hearing more about your seminars and workshops regarding sales, customer service, and human development.

I think we have found out today why you are so successful and why you work so hard. You are truly a Master of Success, and we thank you so much for your pearls of wisdom.

About The Author

From poverty to prosperity and from living a life of quiet desperation to champagne wishes and caviar dreams—this story has changed lives. It is a story of a forty-four-year-long journey that is packed with lack and self-limiting beliefs to extraordinary triumphs and Herculean events. Donna Hickey has inspired people to change, to reach beyond self-limiting beliefs, to live the abundant life, break through fear, and prosper.

Donna Hickey

Phone: 630.585.7477

Email: donna@donnahickey.com

www.donnahickey.com

Chapter Seven

TEA HOFFMANN, ESQ.

THE INTERVIEW

David Wright (Wright)

Today we are talking with Tea Hoffmann, Esq. Tea is president of Legal Training Group, LLC, based in Nashville, Tennessee. She practiced law for more than fourteen years before beginning her business, which is focused on speaking and training lawyers. Tea's personal vision is to help lawyers become what she terms more "E²P²" or "Efficient, Effective, Productive, and Profitable."

Since founding her business in 2001, she has spoken to thousands of attorneys nationwide and has produced training programs for more than fifty law firms. Tea is the founder of The Partnership Institute, an exclusive organization designed to train new law partners to reach and exceed their potential.

Tea is author of *The Proactive Practice: Change Your Practice, Change Your Life* and is currently working on her second book, *The E²P² Principle.*

Tea is the mother of two children, a wife, and a Major in the Tennessee Army National Guard.

Tea Hoffman, welcome to *Masters of Success.*

Tea Hoffmann (Hoffmann)
Thank you for inviting me to be a part of this program.

Wright
So what made you decide to leave the practice of law?

Hoffmann
I had practiced law for more than fourteen years and during that time the practice of law changed significantly. The practice of law shifted from a traditional seller's market to a buyer's market. The shift was caused by several factors, including changes in technology, the number of lawyers in the marketplace and momentous changes in the rules regarding advertising and marketing.

The shift began to manifest itself in the early nineties. At that time, I was general counsel of a publicly traded company in Tennessee. As a client of many law firms, I began to recognize that many law firms were lagging behind in the area of marketing and advertising, client development, and customer care. I also recognized that many of our outside counsels needed to update their technology and recognize that the playing field for law firms had dramatically changed. Firms now faced competition from other firms who were aggressively seeking their client base and many did not know how to face this "new reality."

Understanding what was happening in the marketplace, I decided to develop a company to help train lawyers address this new reality and protect their current client base, which, in my opinion, are their most valuable assets.

Wright
What issues do lawyers face in today's practice of law, and how does your company help them?

Hoffmann
Lawyers are trying to catch up with bankers, accountants, and other professionals who encountered similar issues probably about five years sooner than lawyers.

Most practicing lawyers receive no customer service training, business training, client retention training, client development training, or time management training in law school. Yet, when they get out into the practice of law they're expected to build a book of business, create a profitable practice—either for themselves or the firm in which they work—and they are expected to become a part of many different organizations so that they can begin to build a client base long-term. It's very difficult for them because most don't have the skills necessary unless one or more of those skills comes naturally to them. Even if they have natural ability, they might not be able to properly utilize it. This is where Legal Training Group (LTG) comes in.

Wright

Do you think lack of training is because years ago it was actually against the law, as I understand it, to even advertise? Do you think that has carried over into their mindset?

Hoffmann

I think it certainly has. Advertising is still frowned upon by many lawyers. Lawyers "won the right" to advertising in the late 1980s. Prior to that time, advertising was unethical and lawyers could lose their license to practice if they choose to advertise their trade. In the early 1990s, lawyers began to understand the potential and power that advertising and marketing could bring to their practice.

Today there are still ethical guidelines lawyers must follow if they choose to advertise. These rules are created and governed by individual states and by the American Bar Association. However, these rules are there to protect the public and do not, in general, prohibit lawyers from getting their unique message out to the marketplace.

Wright

So how do these rules safeguard the public?

Hoffman

Lawyers have a unique place in our society. We are professionals and the public expects us to be trustworthy and have the highest level of integrity. For those reasons, lawyers must advertise and market themselves in a manner that projects clearly how they can help their clients without making promises that they cannot keep or representing themselves in an overbroad way. For example, a lawyer can never guarantee a result for a client, nor can a lawyer use terms like "greatest lawyer in America!" as that would be overboard.

Wright

At what point is your company normally hired and specifically, how does your company assist in overcoming the problems lawyers face?

Hoffmann

Unfortunately, our company is usually hired at the point *after* we are needed the most. Many of our firms, especially early in our business, hired us after they had lost a client, when they had begun to lose associates because they are not properly trained, or when they were having a profitability problem. That has changed somewhat in the last two years. We are seeing more firms recognize that they need a clear-cut business strategy and marketing plan and call us for assistance before a problem arises.

Many firms hire us initially to do just training. Our programs are very well done and provide not only excellent content, but also give lawyers tangible ways to accomplish their individual and firm objectives. For example, in our training series titled "Destination Partnership," associates are taught, throughout the eight sessions, how to better manage their time, organize their lives and their offices, communicate better with clients, staff, and peers, how to get and retain clients, and how law firm economics works. This program sometimes leads to the firm's recognition that they need to solidify pieces of this training firm-wide. After conducting this series, for example, we have had firms ask us to come in and institute a client retention plan.

Other programs, like Dr. Tony Alessandra's *Platinum Rule* program, are taught to lawyers at all levels and provide tremendous and long-term benefits. Our company is also certified in several of the FranklinCovey® courses, including the *Focus* course which helps attorneys set goals and manage their time and their lives—something lawyers seem to struggle with greatly. We also offer the *Seven Habits* course which follows along the same guidelines but with a little more breadth to it. Our core group members have also established many of our own courses and curricula that enable lawyers to become more successful. For example, Susan DePue, one of our key core group members, works with clients on marketing strategies. Many times these sessions lead to LTG helping the firm to develop a written marketing plan.

Wright

So you're not teaching them courtroom strategies, you're talking about business principles.

Hoffmann

That's exactly right. Some people would say the things we teach are "soft" substantive skills instead of "hard" substantive skills. We have no courses that teach them how to write a better brief, or argue better in front of a judge. We believe those are skills taught in law school and should be skills that are being mentored by the other lawyers within the law firm environment.

We believe that what is most needed are the things that are going to help lawyers be successful long-term and are not taught in law school or necessarily mentored once a lawyer joins a firm or begins to practice.

Wright

How much of the kinds of things you are trying to teach them are covered by the law schools out there?

Hoffmann

None. Law schools are still focused on what they consider "more substantive" topics. We are trying to market to law schools, but have not penetrated this market yet. Vanderbilt University's law school had us do a session on networking this year. Over 150 students attended the session...so the demand is there. Our job now is to convince other schools to address the demand and understand the need for this type of training.

Wright

Do you cover trust issues in your training? The reason I ask is I always like to really, really trust my attorney who is almost like my doctor. There's no way to arrive at that trust except over the course of time. Do you cover those kinds of issues?

Hoffmann

We cover those issues extensively. One of the programs produced in an online CLE in 2002 was titled, "Developing Clients that Last a Lifetime." This program focused on developing trusting relationships with clients—even friendships—versus just looking at clients as a source of revenue. Client relationships are based on trust. A lawyer may be able to get a new client after just meeting him or her one time, but that is rare. If you want a client to last a lifetime, you must work to develop a relationship with that client and work hard at keeping that relationship viable. Lawyers need to get to know their clients at a deeper level—deeper than just their legal issues. In that way you can help anticipate what their needs are going to be, not only from a business standpoint but also from a personal standpoint. You can begin to develop the trusting relationship that's not only going to enable you to keep that client but will encourage that client to refer other clients to you which, of course, will help you grow your practice.

Wright

Interesting. The layperson doesn't think of law firms as businesses.

Hoffmann

No.

Wright

In your book, *The Proactive Practice*, you talk extensively about the practice of law being a business and the importance of business planning. Why do you consider this is so important to lawyers?

Hoffmann

David, let me ask you this question: If you were asked to invest in a company that didn't have a business or marketing plan, would you invest in that company?

Wright

Nope.

Hoffmann

Well, believe it or not, it has been written that only seven percent of all law firms nationwide have a written business or marketing plan. We have talked with firms that say they have one; they just don't have it written down. Our experience is firms that have their goals and plans written down and that regularly review those and measure themselves against those goals, knowing that those plans must be flexible, are more successful long-term.

It is important for law firms to think like a business with the understanding, of course, that a law firm is still a professional practice. This is certainly a balance and one that many firms are

This is certainly a balance and one that many firms are struggling with. For example, all lawyers should devote some time to pro bono work. This "free" legal work not only helps the client, but expands the lawyer's acumen in areas that they may not have had experience in before. However, law firms want their lawyers to bill hours, as this is how lawyers maximize their profits, and since pro bono work is non-billable, many larger firms struggle with how to strike an appropriate balance. LTG works with firms to help them find the appropriate balance while maximizing profitability.

Wright

Do you believe that success is tied to planning? Or can success be achieved without a solid plan?

Hoffmann

I believe that success is *definitely* tied to planning. As John Wooden said, "failure to plan is planning to fail."

In many of the firms we service, we ask firm partners what their goals are and how they plan to reach them. If we ask ten lawyers, we will get ten different and unique answers. All of these answers are generally plausible and well thought out, but they are different. LTG works with these firms to put those plans down in a cohesive way so that a plan can be written and followed. Then we work with the firm to implement the plan and provide the training to help the firm reach the goals set out in their plan.

Wright

How do you plan to grow your company?

Hoffmann

Our plan currently is to continue extensively working the market segments throughout the U.S.

We are also focused on conducting business over the Internet and coaching over the phone. We expect these offerings to be popular with our solo practitioners and with other market segments we serve. Another focus area is providing continuing legal education programs online. We have nine programs available currently. Lawyers are beginning to use online continuing legal education tools to get their education hours versus attending a seminar. We believe that this is going to be a growth and expansion area for us.

Wright

What products or services do you plan to add in the future?

Hoffmann

We plan to add the second book, *The E²P² Principle,* by the spring of 2006 and we have a third book that will be a collaborative effort between myself and another core group member that we're planning to release in 2006.

We'll be adding another six online continuing legal education (CLE) programs by the end of 2005 year, so that will bring our number to fifteen online CLE programs. In addition, we have twelve programs licensed from a third party that are actually about marketing for professionals. Our plan is to customize those for lawyers.

Wright

I don't know if it went over my head or not, but what in the world is the "E²P² Principle"?

Hoffmann

Efficient, Effective, Productive, and Profitable—this is the core mission of our company—everything has to fall into one or more of those categories. If it's not a program or service that will help make law firms more efficient, more effective, more productive, or more profitable, then it's not something we offer.

Wright

Who is your competition and how are you different?

Hoffmann

We have some competitors who are in the legal training marketplace. I think there are two things that differentiate us. One is that I am a lawyer and we have other lawyers in our core group. We have all worked in law firms and understand the angst lawyers face on a daily basis.

Secondly, I've been a client of law firms. This element differentiates me in particular. I understand, as a former client, what clients really want and need from their outside counsel.

David, there is a third factor as well. I think that our core group concept is a differentiating factor. We put together not only a core group of speakers and trainers, but we add consultants who can work with these firms long-term.

Many consulting firms put together what we call the "big, fat, hairy binder." Participants receive a big binder at the end of a consulting project but they get nothing that helps them utilize the binder. What we do is provide the big binder *and* people who actually stay with the firm on a long-term basis to help them implement the things that are in the binder and train them on how to do the things contained in the binder. From our standpoint, that's really where the "rubber meets the road." If you've got a big binder and no one uses it, you've just thrown your money away.

Wright

In your book, *The Proactive Practice*, you talk extensively about the practice of law being a business and the importance of business planning. Why do you consider this is so important to lawyers?

Hoffmann

David, let me ask you this question: If you were asked to invest in a company that didn't have a business or marketing plan, would you invest in that company?

Wright

Nope.

Hoffmann

Well, believe it or not, it has been written that only seven percent of all law firms nationwide have a written business or marketing plan. We have talked with firms that say they have one; they just don't have it written down. Our experience is firms that have their goals and plans written down and that regularly review those and measure themselves against those goals, knowing that those plans must be flexible, are more successful long-term.

It is important for law firms to think like a business with the understanding, of course, that a law firms is still a professional practice. This is certainly a balance and one that many firms are struggling with. For example, all lawyers should devote some time to pro bono work. This "free" legal work not only helps the client, but expands the lawyer's acumen in areas that they may not have had experience in before. However, law firms want their lawyers to bill hours, as this is how lawyers maximize their profits, and since pro bono work is non-billable, many larger firms struggle with how to strike an appropriate balance. LTG works with firms to help them balance. LTG works with firms to help them find the appropriate balance while maximizing profitability.

Wright

Do you believe that success is tied to planning? Or can success be achieved without a solid plan?

Hoffmann

I believe that success is *definitely* tied to planning. As John Wooden said, "failure to plan is planning to fail."

In many of the firms we service, we ask firm partners what their goals are and how they plan to reach them. If we ask ten lawyers, we will get ten different and unique answers. All of these answers are generally plausible and well thought out, but they are different. LTG works with these firms to put those plans down in a cohesive way so that a plan can be written and followed. Then we work with the firm to implement the plan and provide the training to help the firm reach the goals set out in their plan.

Wright

Tell me about your company and the core group concept.

Hoffmann

What we realized was that speaking and training was a "quick fix" for many law firms. When we went in and did a speech or did a law firm retreat, for example, during a weekend, we got really good results for about sixty days. But what we wanted to do was have an impact that was long-term. What we did was begin to surround ourselves with consultants who did more than just speak and train.

The consultants in our core group go deeper. For example, they go in and help law firms write a business plan, help firms create marketing materials, and help perform personality profiles before the firms hire individuals so they can make sure they are making the right hiring decisions. Our consultants also help with executive coaching in the areas of leadership, marketing, and time management. In essence, we began to put together people who could help implement the solutions we were talking about in our training program.

Wright

On your personality profiling, do you use DiSC® or Myers Briggs®?

Hoffmann

We use HBDI, Herrmann Brain Dominance Instrument® along with Dr. Tony Alessandra's Platinum Rule Profile™.

Wright

That also should help them with customer service, shouldn't it?

Hoffmann

Yes. It definitely helps them with customer service.

Wright

My son used to be an accountant for a major law firm. One of the things they invested in was some pretty sophisticated software for their billing. They would bill out in ten-minute increments. For example, if another attorney from the opposing side wrote a letter, and they read it and answered it, it was billable at ten minutes to read it and maybe ten or twenty minutes to answer it. Keeping track of the time helped the business quite a bit. Do you do things like that?

Hoffmann

LTG has a wonderful legal technology "guru" in our core group. Phillip Hampton specializes in only legal software and technology. He is an incredible asset to our team as law firms have very unique ways of billing, tracking cases, and managing conflicts of interest. In addition, Phillip can help firms prepare a case for trial by offering them the latest technology to help them win their case, and can also help firms by providing computer forensic services.

In addition, Phillip helps train staff and lawyers on how to use the technology they have at their disposal. Phillip can add significant efficiencies to the firms he serves.

Wright

Your company is very niche oriented; do you plan to keep it that way?

Hoffmann

At this point, we do. We have had several opportunities to work with accounting firms and other professional service firms since we began, and we are not opposed to working outside of the legal field at some point in our future. However, at this point, our plan is to focus on the legal sector niche. There are more than 700,000 practicing attorneys in the U.S. so we don't think there's a shortage of lawyers for us to teach. In addition, we have broken that number into market sectors for greater penetration. For example, we have a market sector for solo practitioners, one for small firms (firms of less than twenty lawyers), one for women lawyers, etc. In all, we have identified eleven distinct market sectors that we plan to penetrate. We know that each sector is unique and each of these desire different types of training, services, and products. Our job, and our challenge, is to get our arms around the legal niche's demand before moving into another niche marketplace.

Wright

That many lawyers will keep the comedians up at night just thinking up new jokes!

Hoffmann

I'm glad you brought that up—and you are right! One of the things I constantly remind the lawyers we teach is to be proud of our profession. David, lawyers have a unique place in our society. Lawyers have the ability to change the lives of the clients they serve; they have the ability to change the rules and regulations that govern business by simply trying and winning a case. They also have the ability to change the rules that govern our society. For example, a lawyer, Thurgood Marshall, fought to integrate our schools. Lawyers across this country fight hard every day for their clients and for justice.

The practice of law, while very much a business, is still a profession and as lawyers we should be proud of our profession and never allow others to demean it. I can't tell you how many lawyer jokes I have heard, but I have come to believe that it is the lawyers' job to educate the public about the importance and significance of our profession. That said, as with any profession, there are some bad apples, but there are not very many, and those bad apples tend to be exposed relatively quickly.

Wright

How much of the kinds of things you are trying to teach them are covered by the law schools out there?

Hoffmann

None. Law schools are still focused on what they consider "more substantive" topics. We are trying to market to law schools, but have not penetrated this market yet. Vanderbilt University's law school had us do a session on networking this year. Over 150 students attended the session...so the demand is there. Our job now is to convince other schools to address the demand and understand the need for this type of training.

Wright

One last question: Do you cover trust issues in your training? The reason I ask is I always like to really, really trust my attorney who is almost like my doctor. There's no way to arrive at that trust except over the course of time. Do you cover those kinds of issues?

Hoffmann

We cover those issues extensively. One of the programs produced in an online CLE in 2002 was titled, "Developing Clients that Last a Lifetime." This program focused on developing trusting relationships with clients—even friendships—versus just looking at clients as a source of revenue. Client relationships are based on trust. A lawyer may be able to get a new client after just meeting him or her one time, but that is rare. If you want a client to last a lifetime, you must work to develop a relationship with that client and work hard at keeping that relationship viable. Lawyers need to get to know their clients at a deeper level—deeper than just their legal issues. In that way you can help anticipate what their needs are going to be, not only from a business standpoint but also from a personal standpoint. You can begin to develop the trusting relationship that's not only going to enable you to keep that client but will encourage that client to refer other clients to you which, of course, will help you grow your practice.

Wright

Interesting. The layperson doesn't think of law firms as businesses.

Hoffmann

No.

Wright

What an interesting conversation. I really appreciate the time you have spent with me here. Thank you for all these candid answers. I think you're doing a great job. I've never heard of anything like this, so when I asked you if you had any competition, I'd expected you to say no.

Hoffmann

I wish I *didn't* have any competition! But the competitors we do have are all very good at what they do and only push us to become better.

Wright

Today we have been talking with Tea Hoffmann, Esq., president of the Legal Training Group, LLC. I have found out today, and I hope our readers will find out, that Tea is out doing things that the public appreciates—teaching lawyers how to be more businesslike. I think the public ultimately benefits from the training her company offers.

Thank you so much, Tea, for being with us today on *Masters of Success*.

About The Author

Tea Hoffmann is President of Legal Training Group. She practiced law for over fifteen years before beginning her business that is focused on speaking and training lawyers. Tea's personal mission is to help lawyers become what she calls more "E^{2}P^2" or efficient, effective, productive, and profitable.

Since founding her business in 2001 she has spoken to thousands of attorneys nationwide and has produced training programs for over law fifty law firms. Tea is a founder of The Partnership Institute, an exclusive program designed to train new partners to reach and exceed their potential. Tea is the author of *The Proactive Practice* and is currently working on her second book, titled *The E^{2}P^2 Principle*. Tea is the mother of two children, a wife, and a Major in the Tennessee Army National Guard.

Tea Hoffmann, Esq.

Legal Training Group, LLC

718 Thompson Lane

Ste. 108-203

Nashville, TN 37204

Phone: 888.385.9917

Phone: 615.385.9917

Fax: 615.373.5593

Email: tea@legaltraininggroup.com

www.legaltraininggroup.com

Chapter Eight

MERIT GEST

THE INTERVIEW

David E. Wright (Wright)

Today we're talking with Merit Gest, founder of *Marriage Means Business*. Merit's distinctive method of marrying successful business strategies with personal relationships creates a unique approach to making a marriage work.

As a member of The National Speakers Association, Merit has been invited to speak all across America, including: American Library Association, Microsoft, CBS Radio, and American Express. Merit has trained hundreds of salespeople to collectively increase sales by millions of dollars across a wide variety of industries, though her most treasured "sale" was on her wedding day! Although Merit is not a licensed therapist, people relate to her because she's a real woman making her marriage work every day.

Merit, welcome to *Masters of Success!*

Merit Gest (Gest)

Thank you David!

Wright

Merit, what do you think makes a successful marriage?

Gest

That's an interesting question because there are no standard measurements for success when it comes to marriage. A business is successful when it meets specific criteria such as: profit margin, customer satisfaction ratings, ROI (Return On Investment), and employee retention percentages. It's easy to know if a business is successful because everyone in that business understands the rules of the game in advance. It's all about profit and loss when it comes to business.

It's impossible to be successful in the game of marriage if you don't understand the rules. In marriage, success is based on emotional satisfaction. So a successful marriage is really measured in moments every day, not just on the number of anniversaries. It's not about counting the anniversaries—it's about making the anniversaries count. It's up to *you* to decide if your marriage is successful and happy, based on criteria that work for *you* and not someone else's version of success or happiness.

Having a successful marriage does not mean that two people never argue or disagree. In fact, in business it's understood that there will be problems to solve along the way as a company is growing. In marriage, a couple faces opportunities for eternal problem-solving and if they view their problems as obstacles they're going to have a much harder time overcoming them. As in business, however, if a couple is able to view their problems as a growth opportunity, then they can work better to solve problems together.

A successful marriage is really about working together through disagreements, because ultimately, as a couple, they agree they are better together than apart.

A marriage really works when the two people in a marriage declare that it works for them, they agree together on what their criteria are for a successful marriage, and they measure their results against their own criteria.

It's important to know what your criteria for success in marriage are in the same way that it would be important for business owners to know what their criteria are for good customer service. How would you know if you're succeeding or failing if you don't have standards on which to base your conclusions? Acknowledging and appreciating the 364 days of successful marriage in between each anniversary is really how a successful marriage is built—one day at a time.

Wright

Can anybody have a successful marriage?

Gest

The answer to your question is yes, but I'll tell you an ironic story. One night, as I was fine-tuning my talk on making marriage work, my husband, Dave, and I had a conversation which actually turned into an argument and then back into a discussion, which led me to think, "This marriage is *never* going to work and here I am about to write a book on this stuff!"

No matter what he said, all I heard was one of his opening comments which was, "I feel like we're just roommates and I think I like it that way. It's easier to do my own thing than to have to deal with you." Ouch! Rather than processing that new insight I turned away from him and mentally decided, "If he wants a roommate, then he'll get a roommate!" I made a mental checklist of all the wonderful things I do for him that I would no longer do if I were going to be downgraded to "roommate" status. I prepared to make him beg me to go back to "wife" status and to do all those "lovey-dovey" things again. I was ready for the fight.

We went to sleep without our ritual kiss goodnight and when we woke the next morning, instead of "good morning honey," I didn't even give a courtesy grunt. I mean there was nothing—no kiss, no "have a good day"—no communication at all. (I remember being more friendly to my roommates.) The entire day went by and all I could think of was, "It's easier just to be roommates. It's easier just to be roommates." I played the conversation over and over in my head. I decided I would plot my course to convince him that being roommates was not what he wanted.

Then it hit me—my plans, my recent behavior—all of it was inconsistent with my true commitment to make my marriage work. If I was going to create a loving marriage it wasn't going to come about by not kissing my husband in the morning and making him feel bad for making me feel bad. I wasn't creating the marriage that I wanted. I was acting like a victim, which was really the only way I could think of to regain control. I wanted to make him realize he was wrong for saying, "It would be easier to just be roommates," rather than looking at myself and what *I* was doing that caused him to feel that way. I was about to ruin my marriage and justify it by saying he's the one who said blah, blah, blah. Naturally, I would have gotten away with it, because as long as I told people who would support my side, as opposed to making me take responsibility, I would be okay.

It wasn't the easier choice in the initial moment, but instead of trying to hurt him in retaliation of my feeling hurt I decided to interact with Dave as if I was already creating a wonderful marriage with him. I even apologized for how I ended the day and started the next day. I told him that I was committed to our marriage and not committed to living under the same roof as a roommate. I told him I was taking full responsibility for it being *easy* and *phenomenal* to be married to me. His face just lit up—he was missing our connection too.

We both agreed that we had to make some adjustments in our self-involved lives to include each other. By my taking responsibility for our marriage, I made it easy for him to take responsibility as well.

After the "roommate incident," as we now refer to it, we started going out on more dates—just the two of us. We had dinner together without the television and we went to bed earlier so we could enjoy our time to reconnect. As two self-involved people it was a burden to make time for each other since it took time away from what we were trying to accomplish on our own. Once the roommate incident made it clear that we were headed down the path toward a loveless marriage, we were able to talk it through and re-create what we really wanted for our marriage *and it happened in a moment.*

The moment I made the decision to honor my true commitment and not be the selfish little girl who got hurt, my marriage was changed forever. You can't let those juicy moments pass you by. It only takes one person who is totally committed to making their marriage work to recognize when you're in a downward spiral and then to take charge and alter that course. One person can shift the direction in a moment. A successful marriage is measured in *those* moments.

Wright

So why is it important to you that people have a successful marriage?

Gest

Marriage, as an institution, is not working. We've all heard the statistics that fifty percent of all marriages end in divorce and whether that's an accurate percentage or inflated is really irrelevant. The fact is it's not ten percent. There are some marriages that really are not good partnerships and should be ended for various reasons such as abuse, infidelity, and addiction which are major issues beyond the scope of what I'm qualified to discuss. The problem is that good people in good marriages are calling it quits too soon.

When I work with entrepreneurs I see the same scenario over and over again. Highly qualified experts leave their employers to open their own business. They hang their shingles out and wonder why their phones aren't ringing. They then discover that they have to go out and get the business. That's when they separate themselves into two groups. Some entrepreneurs close their doors and go back to work for someone else and other entrepreneurs learn how to get business and then enjoy building their own company.

The same trend is happening in marriage. Some people enter into a marriage and when it starts to get tough they shut down and get out. Other people learn what they need to learn to deal with the tough times and they renew their commitment to tough it out together.

I have something to say about making marriage work based on what I've learned and what I've taught people who are committed to making their businesses work. There's just too much resignation out there and not enough commitment and responsibility. I'm here to say that *anything* is possible if you bring your commitment to it and you're willing to do whatever it takes to make it work.

When we get married we agree, "Until death do us part," though in reality I've seen people do more to keep their businesses going than to keep their marriage going. Perhaps if we thought about marriage as a corporation we would have a different connection with the idea of marriage. "Until death do us part" can kill you or it can inspire you; and how you relate to the promise you made to your spouse will be the deciding factor.

My parents were divorced when I was a child and after hearing the stories about their fairytale wedding it was shocking to learn that they were calling it quits. The message I got was that someday, if I did get married, I would never really know if it would work out even if I started with my own storybook wedding ceremony.

Aren't we all afraid of the unknown? Early in my marriage I was consumed by fear that my husband would decide he didn't want to be married to me anymore and we would get divorced. Then later I imagined my son crying in his room, like I did when I was a child, with only his teddy bears to console him. I felt like a victim—I was unable to control my destiny and unable to control my ability to stay happily married. It got worse. I then started to panic that my worrying about the possibility of being divorced might actually create a self-fulfilling prophecy, in spite of the fact that I had no evidence of a reason for us to split up. Imagine—my being worried that my husband would cheat on me would actually be the very thing that would drive him away!

What was bothering me most was the feeling of insecurity and uncertainty. I remember feeling that way when I was single. I teased myself that once I was married the insecurities and uncertainties about men and relationships and "forever" would disappear the moment I heard "I do" and kissed the guy. What I wasn't prepared for was that the uncertainty really got more intense. I now knew exactly what I would be missing if my marriage got screwed up. I now knew how deeply I could love a man and be loved by a man. I now knew that I didn't want to be without this man. When you're not certain of what will come, the uncertainty is one thing; but uncertainty when you fear losing what you've got is quite another.

When I'm uncertain about big business deals, I build a plan, I review my notes, I ask for coaching, and I practice what I'm going to say. I take responsibility and I do whatever I can to win the business. When I felt uncertainty in my relationships, I didn't quite know what to do because I didn't think I could control the outcome. Why not just use the same skills and techniques that worked successfully in business to help my marriage last?

I made a choice: I could spend the rest of my life worrying that someday I would get divorced, or I could spend the rest of my life choosing to have a great marriage every day—enjoy every moment, *in* the moment. I built a plan and practiced being a better partner in the relationship.

Rather than blaming stupid prospects or difficult economic times when sales don't close, top producers look first at themselves to see what they could or should have done differently in the situation. Excuse-makers are busy blaming other people; winners take responsibility. Your prospects don't have to change to do business with you.

Your spouse also doesn't have to change to stay married to you. You married your spouse as is and there is a reason the two of you chose each other. There's something for both of you to learn from each other. It's not always comfortable, but if you ask yourself what you can get out of the experience, good or bad, you'll be better equipped for the next situation.

I'm clear that everything I've learned and studied to be successful in business through books, seminars, therapy, transformational work, coaching, and tears has made a positive difference in my marriage. When I started to apply the same principles I teach sales people on how to grow their business to growing my marriage, I noticed a dramatic positive shift in my relationship. Just as people experience a positive increase by using proper mindsets, actions, and tools, I've experienced an enhanced marriage using those same principles.

Wright

Would you give us an example of a sales technique couples can use to create a better marriage?

Gest

I can give you several. In sales there's a widely held theory that the problem the prospect brings you is never the real problem. The job of a professional sales person is to ask the right questions to get to the heart of the issue. Asking questions is the only way to really qualify or disqualify a prospect. So, let me give you an example of how this theory works in a relationship.

One night I came home after conducting an all-day training class and my husband came downstairs and saw me in the kitchen. The first words out of his mouth were, "Have you started making dinner yet?" Now, as you can imagine, I had an automatic response to that kind of question, especially after a long day. Fortunately, I had taught the group the importance of finding out why a question is being asked and how *that* is often more important than answering the question. Instead of responding with, "Are you crazy? I just worked hard all day and that's the greeting I get? Make it yourself!" I was able to ask, "What's on your mind?" To which he responded, "Well last night you mentioned you would be training all day so I thought you might be tired and I'd take you out for dinner."

It's really critical to understand why your spouse is asking the questions he or she is asking. When Dave, says, "Do we have plans on Saturday?" I know that's not the real issue. The real issue is, "I want to go out with the guys," or, "I want to take you out," or something like that. Instead of asking a direct question, many people dance around the real issue. Getting to the *real* issue underneath the question being asked is a critical skill for men and women to master, both in business and in personal relationships. When you understand the intent behind the question you and your spouse will be able to communicate much more effectively.

Here's another example: Sales is often a relationship business. Without the proper foundation of strong rapport it's very difficult for salespeople to close deals. Building rapport is a critical step—not just early in the sales process but throughout the relationship. Back in "Sales 101," training and textbooks taught people to pick out something familiar in a prospect's office and get them talking about it. We were taught to make small talk about weather, traffic, sports, or a picture on the client's desk. The problem with small talk is that it doesn't create rapport because it's really just "fluffy" conversation. It never distinguishes you from your competitors who are typically talking about the same topics.

Professional sales people don't fall into that small talk trap; they create much stronger rapport through subconscious means using tools such as Neuro-Linguistic Programming (NLP). NLP has been around for years and basically it's about communicating with another person in the manner that's comfortable for them in terms of how they process information.

NLP divides people into three categories: visual, auditory, and kinesthetic. To communicate most effectively with visual people you might draw a picture or include a graph in your presentation. Auditory people respond well to the words you choose and the tonality that you use. Kinesthetic people trust their instinct or focus on feelings and learn through experience and action. Communicating with another person in the way they are most comfortable and receptive is one of the things that separates high producing business professionals from the rest of the pack.

When you understand the power of NLP it works for you in a very profound way. When you don't understand how NLP works, it works against you and you're really left scratching your head wondering why things didn't work out.

Now let's apply this principle to your marriage. I'm a very visual person—I think in pictures. I'm constantly doodling and I'm much better with faces than names. My husband is visual as well, but he tends to be slightly more auditory in his style. He prefers the phone to e-mail, says something once and expects it to sink in, and he remembers stacks of details from most conversations.

Every month we go through our budget and we take a look at where our money was spent during the past month and what we're budgeting for in the future. When we first started reviewing our finances, Dave would talk to me about the numbers he analyzed. We were trying to allocate money to buy some investments so he was explaining verbally how much we put in "this pot" and how much is going into "that pot." Try as I might, I did not get it. I'm no accounting wiz, but I'm not an idiot either. The way he was explaining it just did not compute. He would say the same things over and over and in different ways, but it still didn't register with me. Finally, he got out one of the flip charts I use for training and he drew me a picture. Instantly, I understood what he had been desperately trying to explain for a solid hour.

It's really important to know how your spouse processes information so you can communicate in a way that he or she is most likely to understand. Listen to the clues that are given when he or she speaks. Are words used such as "show me," or "paint the picture," or, "how do I look?" If those terms are used or your spouse tends to use a lot of gestures while communicating, then he or she is most likely a visual communicator. Does your spouse enjoy music with dinner or call you frequently, or say "Tell me you love me," or describe situations using words such as "hear," "sound," or "listen"? If so, he or she is probably more auditory. When your partner chooses to describe his or her feelings or say how much he or she likes to be held and if he or she learns from taking lessons rather than reading books, your spouse is probably more kinesthetic.

Pay attention to how your partner communicates with you. You'll be far more effective in your communication if you speak in his or her visual, auditory, or kinesthetic language.

Wright

What kind of example can you give our readers about how you and your husband use a specific business technique to keep your love alive?

Gest

When Dave and I were dating, I kept a secret journal. I wrote in the journal after we'd talk on the phone or when I came home from a date. The actual entry on August 16, 1999 reads, "Even as in love as we are, you can't make any guarantees. I bet each day as long as we live I could come up with a totally different reason why I love you. In fact, I bet it would be really, really easy. Hey, that gives me a good idea—a calendar—just a date and a blank line and every day I would fill in a new reason I came up with to love you that day." Well that is exactly how the *When I Fell In Love With You Today*™ calendar was born.

Too often an entire day goes by and we haven't felt appreciated or loved. When too many of those days go by, we wake up one morning and wonder if there's more to life than what we have and we start to notice what else is out there that we may perceive to be better.

Borrowing a lesson from the sales methodology I've been teaching for almost ten years, I know that clients leave because they don't feel they are valued or that their business is appreciated. Relationships are no different. People really look to satisfy their need for appreciation every day. If you're not appreciated at home you might look for *that* need to be met with clients, prospects, coworkers, alcohol, shopping, drugs—the list is endless. You may feel under-appreciated at work so you would look to someone at home to make up the difference. People who feel appreciated in one area take that healthy self-esteem with them to other areas of their life.

If you have a high feeling of self-worth you're more likely to perform at a high level in each of the roles you play. It's really important for a healthy marriage and a fulfilling life that people feel appreciated every single day.

Every night before Dave and I turn off the lights, we write a sentence or two about that moment during the day when we fell in love with each other again. I have five years worth of calendars containing new reasons my husband and I have discovered to love each other every single day. We have skipped a few days—we are human. Sometimes the reasons are silly; other times profound. Most of the time they're moments that really would have slipped by unnoticed. With the *When I Fell In Love With You Today*™ calendar they're captured, recorded, easily remembered, and shared. We love going back to past calendars and reliving moments when we fell in love with each other.

When I'm working with business professionals I teach them to journal—write down the lessons they've learned so they can go back to them and see how far they've come and see what they've learned every day in business.

Wright

Is there anything you wish you would have known before you got married?

Gest

I wish I would have *believed* the people who told me that marriage takes some effort. I wish I would have known that couples who I think are as happy as can be argue. I wish I would have known that it doesn't have to be a problem to argue as long as both people are committed to making the marriage work in spite of whatever may come their way. I wish someone had told me that I could create my marriage as long as I'm willing to be responsible for it being phenomenal. I wish somebody had reminded me that everything worthwhile is worth the investment of time and attention. We've all heard the saying, "Rome wasn't built in a day," and I wish that somebody had told me that a successful marriage is built one day at a time.

When I wanted to establish myself in my career, I read books, attended seminars, enrolled mentors to coach me, and did whatever else was necessary to ensure that I would be successful in business. I wish I had taken care of my marriage earlier on with the same care and attention with which I treated my growing business. I wish I had paid more attention to business lessons I learned and applied them earlier to my marriage. But, if you ask me what I do, now that I *am* married, it's simple—*I stay committed.* I make my marriage a consistent focus. I'm always learning how to be a better wife for my husband and partner in our marriage and I take responsibility for my marriage being phenomenal.

Wright

Can you give me at least one tip to make my marriage work better? I've been married for twenty-eight years and it's time I renewed it a little bit. Maybe you can tell me how I can do this.

Gest

I love that you want to renew it after that length of time; I think that's terrific! First, you have to decide that your marriage will work and you are totally committed to making it work. Second, you have to get started *right now.* Surprise your wife with a gesture, a comment, or an action that lets her know you appreciate her and you're committed to her no matter what—and communicate in *her* language.

Next time you're arguing, really listen to your spouse. Listen to her point of view, take a step back and see if she really does have a point. See if you can allow yourself to experience what it must be like for her in that moment, desperately trying to get through to you. Listen from your "commitment to making your marriage work" rather than your "ego trying to win an argument."

The coaching I give salespeople who are fed up with results at a certain level and are desperate to improve their results is no different. First, I tell them that it's time to decide they're responsible for everything they have and everything they don't have. Then, we work together to create a plan so they can get into action immediately. I tell them to listen to their prospects so they don't miss opportunities to do more business together or retain an account that may have been headed out the door.

If you want your wife to hear your points, make sure you are listening to hers. In business, if sales people are doing too much talking it means they're not doing enough listening. Sales are made when salespeople are listening. Highly effective sales professionals are really "smooth listeners," not "smooth talkers."

Fighting to be right almost killed my marriage in the first two years. At the end of the day it's really not that important to win the fight. What's important is to listen to each other and be strong enough to give up your fight to be right, because it takes an unshakeable commitment in the toughest of times to say, "You've got a point honey, I hear you." In those moments when you hear your spouse, you allow him or her the space to hear you as well.

It only takes one person to be committed to making it work. It may take two to tango, but it only takes one to stop an argument. When one person, acting out of his or her commitment to the marriage takes a step back, removes himself/herself from the situation headed in a downward spiral, then *that* person is making a difference in the future of the relationship. If nobody is open, able, or willing to stop the action, then be prepared for a long bumpy ride down the spiral.

Wright

How did your marriage change when you started applying the business strategies you teach to your relationship?

Gest

When I looked at my husband as if he was a hot prospect, I decided to build a plan to get and keep his business. I looked at the behaviors I would do on a consistent basis to get the results I wanted, much like I followed an action plan to pursue prospects and keep in touch with clients. I really listened to my husband and I used the questioning techniques I had been teaching salespeople to get to the intent of the question and deal with the real issues. It was also important to create and build on the rapport we had established early on. As I've taught people how to network effectively, I've taught myself how to create instant rapport and keep it going with my husband. My marriage changed the moment I decided I was not going to be a victim of a marriage that was just okay—I was going to create a marriage that was phenomenal!

Wright

Did he feel the change?

Gest

Absolutely. The more I treated the marriage as seriously as I treated my business, the easier it was for him to treat the marriage seriously, which gave us a much more fulfilling marriage and piece of mind that the relationship would last no matter what problems came up.

Wright

So what is the one message you would like people to be left with?

Gest

I want people to have a sense of confidence that it is possible to create the marriage they want and that the first step is for them to decide to make it work. Most business professionals have a very clear idea of what they can and should do to keep their jobs. Imagine approaching marriage and family as if it was a business partnership. Once we learn what we could and should do to keep our "job," then we will be able to take responsibility for making it a success. It's easy to fail if you don't know the criteria for success.

Making a marriage work doesn't have to be work—you don't need to be a Ph.D. to be a great Mr. or Mrs. In marriage it's not that people *can't* make it work, it's that they've accepted a level of workability or non-workability that's appropriate for the level of knowledge they currently have about themselves, their partner, and their relationship. To make it work better, you have to learn *more* about what makes marriage work and what your role *is* in making it phenomenal, so that you can do something about it.

Wright

What a great conversation! In this idea you have of relating marriage to business you bring up some great thoughts. I'm going to study this chapter of the book and see how I can use this information in my own marriage.

Gest

If I can just add one other thing, David.

Wright

Certainly.

Gest

I work on my marriage every day and I'm just like you—I'm an everyday person. Every day I check in with my husband to make sure we have created and captured moments so that we can call it a "successful marriage day." I'm not a certified, accredited, licensed therapist, psychiatrist, or psychologist. I don't have a Ph.D. and I didn't go to an Ivy League school. My only credentials for talking about this topic are that I am successful in the business world and I am using those same skills to create a successful marriage. I am committed to passing along the shortcuts I've learned to others who are committed to doing the same. Basically I'm a mid-western woman who loves her husband, her child, and her career. At the end of the day I'm really just like you.

Wright

Today we have been talking with Merit Gest. Founder of *Marriage Means Business*, Merit's distinctive method of marrying successful business strategies with personal relationships creates a unique approach to making a marriage work. As she said, she's not a licensed therapist but I think she knows a whole lot about making marriages work—at least *I'm* going to listen to her.

Merit, thank you so much for being with us today on *Masters of Success!*

About The Author

Merit Gest, founder of "Marriage Means Business" married successful business strategies with personal relationships to create a unique approach to making marriage work. As a member of the National Speakers Association, Merit has been invited to speak all across America including: American Library Association, Microsoft, CBS Radio, and American Express. Merit has trained hundreds of salespeople to collectively increase sales by millions of dollars across a wide variety of industries, though her most treasured "sale" was on her wedding day. Though not a licensed therapist, people relate to Merit because she's a real woman making her marriage work every day.

Merit Gest

Marriage Means Business, Inc.

13152 S. Cicero Avenue, PMB 198

Crestwood, IL 60445-1470

Phone: 877-MmeansB (877-663-2672)

Fax: 866.806.7872

Email: Merit@MarriageMeansBusiness.com

www.MarriageMeansBusiness.com

Chapter Nine

DARREN LaCROIX

David Wright (Wright)

What would you say to someone who wasn't funny, had severe stage fright, and told you they wanted to be a comedian? Darren La-Croix was not a class clown. In fact, in high school he was considered *least likely to ever be funny*. What is worse, when he told his family about his dream of becoming a comedian, it was the first time they ever laughed at something he said. He wasn't kidding. Not only did he go on to become a professional comedian, but he also took his story all the way to the World Championship of Public Speaking. In 2001, out of 25,000 contestants from fourteen countries, Darren LaCroix was crowned the World Champion of Public Speaking.

Darren LaCroix, welcome to *Masters of Success*.

How would you define a master of success?

Darren LaCroix (LaCroix)

God did not give me the gift of making people laugh; he gave me the persistence to learn how. Most people quit too soon.

Success means different things to different people. Each of us measures success differently. A homeless person may see anyone with a good job as a success. Someone with a good job may see anyone with a great family as a success.

Success to me is knowing what you want and figuring out how to get it. We all have successes, though not all of us see them that way.

Mastery is the tough part. I believe mastery is about craving betterment, without getting bored, complacent, or detoured by the words of others. I call those naysayers *success suckers*.

I believe a *master of success* is someone who has figured out a process and learned how to apply it to different areas of life.

I'm a slow learner, but I finally figured out my process. Experience taught me that for me, my process is to *decide* what I want, *sponge off* "the best," be *willing to fail*, and *crave feedback* all the way.

Becoming a comedian was incredibly difficult, but most people thought that for *me* it was impossible. I took the same process that helped me become a comedian and figured out how to replicate it when I aimed for the World Championship of Public Speaking.

Wright

What possessed you to think you could become a comedian when you weren't funny and had severe stage fright?

LaCroix

Well, I had a failing business, was on the verge of financial failure, and had made a proposal of marriage that was rejected. Things were so bad that I had to get a part-time job just to pay *my* employees. I was ready to quit life when one of my buddies, Jim, gave me a motivational tape. On the way to my job one day I listened to it, and heard Brian Tracy ask the question, "What would you dare to dream if you knew you wouldn't fail?" Wow, that was deep to me, especially at that moment in my life. My first thought was, I'd be a comedian. Then the little voice in my head piped up, "But you're not funny, Darren." That little *success sucker* we all have inside of us was right. I'm not funny. But that wasn't the question. The question was not what was I good at, what did I have a natural talent for, or anything like that. It's a good thing I never let my life hinge on my high school aptitude test.

At this point in my life I figured I had nothing to lose. What moved me to give it a shot was not a *dream* to become a comedian, it was to escape regret later in life. I did not want the regret of not trying—or worse, trying half-heartedly and wondering, down the road, what if?

Wright

How do you deal with naysayers, or as you call them, *success suckers?*

LaCroix

My best advice to anyone is, if you have a dream or a goal that seems crazy, don't go to your family for inspiration!

My family loves me but did not believe I could become a comedian, because they thought they knew my personality and did not find me humorous. See, that's the part that stinks. They were trying to help me save face, but they did not understand that being a comedian was a skill that could be learned. When I told them of my idea they compared me to Jerry Seinfeld. Measuring someone just starting out against someone at the top of this profession is not a valid assessment.

My family had never been to a comedy show, never met a comedian, nor did they have any idea about what it took, yet they thought they were qualified to advise me on the subject.

You see, my brother and my cousin are both very funny. At family functions, when the mood is right, they can keep the whole room in stitches. I never could, and still can't. However, you could not hand them a microphone and send them up on stage at a comedy club to make strangers laugh. That is a different skill set—a skill set I learned from someone who was actually doing it.

What I did right was to go to a comedy club, watch a show, and ask a comedian for advice. He told me two things: go watch an amateur night and get a certain book on the subject of writing and performing stand-up comedy. I did both, because I had the *"farmer's attitude,"* which I'll tell you about in a minute.

When I went to the open-mike night I saw other people go up for their first time, and they were horrible. The sight was both painful and intriguing. That inspired me, literally. I compared myself to *that*. I thought, *that* I could do!

Wright

You could be horrible.

LaCroix

Exactly, because I was good at it. I had "horrible" down cold. The best advice on this subject came when I took a class in comedy television writing from an award-winning writer, Stanley Ralph Ross. In class, Stan watched a piece of my work called, "It's Bob's Remote," a skit I did with some of my friends. After class I asked him whether I "had what it took." I wanted to know if my effort was in vain, especially since I'd have to battle the naysayers. Stan said, "Darren, people are going to tell you, you suck. That's part of it."

Now I understand what he meant. It is a process, and all along the way people will tell you that you are crazy. So when people told me I couldn't be funny, it actually inspired me. I thought to myself, there's another one who "just doesn't get it." Stan changed my thought process dramatically. The people who would have burned me out simply added fuel to my fire. I saw that I was making progress, though often it didn't feel that way.

Wright

Did you have any successes early in life that you learned from?

LaCroix

That's easy, high school football. This story, however, has nothing to do with our team record. I love football, but in high school I was only five-foot-eight, 140 pounds, not aggressive, and not very good. My first three years of high school football I sat on the bench, or as we called it, "rode the pine."

Going into my senior year I was mad as heck and not going to take it anymore. I *decided* I had had enough. I was going to do whatever it took not to embarrass myself any more. I believe more people have to make a commitment to themselves, understand there will be bumps, and stick to their commitment anyway. My big brother tried to toughen me up and taught me what lifting weights "really" meant. I started running four miles per day and went to Holy Cross College Football Camp. (Most people on my team did not go to such lengths.) I discovered that it's easy to be noticed by leaders when you care more and work harder than everyone else. So I worked even harder.

When the football season began I still was not a "starter," but I just dug in deeper. By the fourth game I was officially a starting corner back and returning punts. I also got the nickname of "Chester," because I went from a complete wimp to having a remarkable physique. (I need to learn that one over again.) All of it came from doing more than most others were willing to do.

To most people this may not seem like a huge success, but to me it was. All of us have had success in our lives in different areas, but I believe we fail to look back and ask ourselves *why* we succeeded and how we can repeat that success.

I finally learned that self-responsibility is an essential life skill. I truly wish that others would take inventory of their own successes, look back to see the path they took to get there, and apply that wisdom to what they are doing now. We all need to learn what works for us in our own lives.

Whenever I start something I still have to remind myself on a regular basis that I must *decide* to succeed and understand there will be mistakes along the way. It's part of the process.

Wright

What do you think are the biggest obstacles people face in trying to become successful?

LaCroix

That's easy—their own thoughts.

Successful people *think* differently.

When I asked David Brooks, the 1990 World Champion, for advice, he pointed out that people who've never competed in the speech contest will give you advice that's the exact opposite of the advice given by the people who have won.

We need to learn to *think* like the people who are successful doing whatever it is that *we* want to be successful at doing. The thought process comes first; the habits and talents will follow.

When I *decided* to do stand-up comedy, I went to successful comedians and asked them what is important to them; what their "thought process" is.

The World Championship of Public Speaking is a speech contest with six levels. My decision to enter the contest was not to win, but to *perfect* the stories I was already telling in my keynote speeches. My comedy mentors had taught me it is not about writing new material but *perfecting* what you have—making it so good that people are willing to pay to hear it. In 2001 I still had a day job and was working hard to market myself as a speaker. I never took time to *master* my material. I joined the contest to force myself to perfect my own stories.

Many people join the competition with the goal of winning, and when they are not successful they are completely depressed. Many have aspirations of speaking professionally, and probably improve greatly as a result of their hard work and the education they collect along the journey. They see the prize as the trophy. The true prize is their improvement, especially if speaking is what they want to do for a living.

In the speaking world, most bookings come from direct referrals. In other words, someone saw them on stage and said we need *that* speaker for our company. When I'm hired and paid for speaking it's never because of the beautiful piece of Lucite sitting on my mantle. If people who enter competitions view the trophy as the prize, they should just go down to their local trophy shop and buy one. It's a whole lot less hassle.

After I won the first two levels of the contest, I sought coaching from someone who had won the District competition (level four). And after I won the Regional competition (level five), I went to past World Champions and *sponged off them.*

Later, when I decided to be a master at creating educational tools to teach others what I learned, I went to the best in that category and *sponged off them.* One of my mentors recommended an audio by someone who was a master at creating educational tools. I got the tape and listened to it over and over, until that presenter's knowledge and wisdom became part of my thought process. Today, most of my income comes from educational tools, and I teach others how to create such tools as well.

Wright

What did you learn from one of your mentors that still resonates with you today?

LaCroix

My favorite is what I call my $3,500 lesson. It came from a mentor who had a gambling problem, and I let him borrow $3,500 dollars—which I never got back.

He taught me that in comedy, success is all about "stage time." It is not the writing and not the practicing, but it's the actual time you spend facing a live audience. He said it is not how well you do today—it is if you go on stage today, you will be better on stage next week. That's because you have more experience. At the beginning of a comedy career, performing is not a lot of fun, because the audiences are horrible and your material is still being worked on.

One night during a show we were standing at the back of a comedy club and my mentor noticed that I had taken to heart his earlier advice about getting stage time. He said to me, "Darren, I'm a headliner.

I get to play all of the best clubs in New England. I will give you five minutes of stage time wherever I play." He paused, and I got very excited thinking that now I could perform in *real* comedy shows. Then he looked me dead in the eye and finished, "But if I ever offer you stage time and you *ever* refuse, I will never help you again." Ouch!

What his words did for me was to change my thought process. Any time I didn't want to stand up in front of a tiny, drunken audience, sitting and watching would become more painful than going up and bombing. I never turned down *stage time* again.

I used to drive two and a half hours to Portland, Maine, and back in the same night, just for five minutes of *stage time,* which I performed free! At the time, my buddies thought I was stupid. Now I get to fly around the world. I've been to Singapore four times this year and I get paid extremely well for a one-hour speech. I'm considered *lucky.* Apparently you can go from stupid to lucky.

When my mentors in the comedy world drilled *stage time* into me, I started looking anywhere and everywhere for opportunities. Comedy clubs are open only at night, so I started looking for places where I could be in front of audiences during the day. I was sitting at my "day job" when an employee newsletter came across my desk about this thing called Toastmasters. The company I worked for had a corporate Toastmasters club. I had no idea what to expect but thought it might be a great place to get *stage time* without the comedy club bookers seeing me make mistakes. Right away I noticed something different between Toastmasters and the comedy clubs. There were about twelve people in the room, and they were all warm, encouraging, and sober! It was perfect. A great place to screw up! I immediately joined four Toastmasters clubs. I was excited to quadruple my "failure rate."

Why is this my $3,500 lesson? I latched on to advice about stage time. It is crystal clear to me that going up on stage every chance I could, fighting every fiber of my body that told me I should not, was the one discipline that took me from chump to World Champ.

I used to be scared to death of flying. Yet flying became essential to my new job as a speaker. I used to pray and grasp the arm-rest for dear life whenever we encountered even the slightest turbulence. It took a while, but the more "air time" I got, the more my fear went away. Now I can fall asleep before we even take off.

I never did see my money again, but the lesson I learned in losing that $3,500 was more than worth it, and I'd pay it again in a minute. It was worth every penny.

My challenge to anyone who wants to be successful is: what is your *stage time* and how are you going to commit to it and stick with it?

Wright

What is essential for people to succeed?

LaCroix

It depends on what they want to be successful at and, of course, on their own definition of success.

My first night on stage as a comedian I got one little laugh, but even that was a mistake. I'd been reacting to my own disaster on stage. In the eyes of the audience I bombed. Yet I viewed the experience very differently. I knew that in five minutes of stage time I delivered one line that got the desired result (a laugh), though it was not part of my routine. I knew that if I got rid of everything else and figured out how to reproduce the one thing that worked I could do this! I've been doing stand-up comedy ever since that night in Boston, 1992.

I do believe you need mentors. I believe the saddest thing is seeing people working *really* hard in the wrong direction. You need to latch onto the words of mentors and don't let go.

Have you ever had someone's words pop into your head right when you were about to make a bad decision? When I was ready to quit (which I almost did three times) I kept hearing in my head the words of wisdom from Otis Williams, Jr., 1993 World Champion of Public Speaking. He said, "Be so good, the only question is who comes in second."

And from David Brooks, the 1990 World Champion of Public Speaking, who advised me, "Let no one out-prepare you."

These words kept me moving forward every time I wanted to give up or thought my speech wasn't good enough.

Wright

What was one of your biggest failures and what did you learn from it?

LaCroix

Well, are you a farmer or an MBA?

My biggest failure has to be when I owned my own Subway Sandwich shop. I still do jokes about it on stage. I went for the American dream and bought a franchise a year after I graduated college. I don't want to sound like I'm bragging, but I took a $60,000 debt and in just six months I doubled that debt! I turned Subway into a non-profit organization.

I tried to look for the lesson in that, and when I forced myself I found it. When you purchase a franchise they send you to Subway University. There they teach you their "system." In class they taught us the difference between the most successful franchisees and the worst franchisees. The only reason a bank was willing to lend money to someone without business experience was because of the incredible track record of the franchiser. Did you know, at the time, about ninety-eight percent of Subway franchises succeeded? Guess where that left me?

The most successful franchisees were people who were formerly farmers. They understood the ethics of hard work, and they understood that they knew nothing about running a sub shop. They followed the system to the letter. Whatever they were told to do they did, without questioning it.

MBAs and people who previously owned their own businesses were the exact opposite. Once they purchased "the system" they immediately tried to change it. It didn't matter to them that there were 5,000 stores across the country doing it one way, they felt they knew better than "the system."

I'm not saying being an MBA is bad, but without practical experience in a particular industry that is only a beginning. I firmly believe that the MBAs could have been more successful if they'd used the system they were taught, and down the road added their own ideas. Most of us are not that patient. I had started with the attitude of the MBA, not the farmer.

Why did I fail? I failed because of my attitude in thinking that I knew better, though I did not have the practical experience. As adult learners we stink! We want to be better parents so we buy a book on the subject, and as we are reading the advice from an expert we are thinking, "I wouldn't do that—that's stupid!" Well, why did you buy the book if you weren't open to learning?

This point was reinforced by what happened the year after I'd won the World Championship of Public Speaking. I was invited back to speak at the Regional conference (level five in the competition). Everyone from my region knew I was giving a presentation on what I had learned to win the previous year. In my region there were eight contestants. Guess how many came to hear me? Four at most. That's it. That was crazy! The year before, when the speaker was a former

World Champion Mark Brown, I sat in the front row and sponged all I could.

Three contestants at the Regional level in the race for the 2002 championship asked me for advice. One gentleman, Terry, asked me to come watch his speech several times to give him feedback. I did. Jan called me on the phone a few times, and another contestant asked me a question or two via e-mail. Guess what order they came in during the contest? One, two, and three, and it had nothing to do with my advice. Which one do you think worked hardest? I believe it was directly proportional to each one's *farmer's attitude*. Go to the best, get the advice, and don't question it. When you aim for success in any area, do you have the attitude of a farmer?

Wright

What *did* you have going for you?

LaCroix

Being clueless! I *knew* that I did not *know*. So I did what seemed logical—I went to *the best* and did what they told me to. I did not question their advice.

Most people are so concerned with what other people think that they can't bear the thought of admitting they need to learn something. People need to be comfortable with themselves as a person to truly be a good student. I love asking the question, "Are you confident enough to be humble?"

I was comfortable with being clueless. I was an eager student. Who would someone rather teach, an eager student, or people who think they already know it all?

My brother is a pilot. As soon as he saved up the money he went to ground school in Florida to learn from one of the best, a teacher who had logged thousands of hours flying. My brother told me it was one of the best things he ever did. Most aviators, after getting their pilot's license, go immediately for their instructor's license. They do this so that students will pay for some of their own expensive flight time. Think about that. You are learning from someone who recently got his or her own pilot's license. They are just a half step ahead of you. Does that make sense? They can't teach from years of wisdom. Instead of merely following the lessons in a textbook, experienced pilots emphasize what is actually most important.

I know that when I coach speakers, I see things much differently than I did just a few years earlier. Why would you learn from someone just a little ahead of you? That is why I went to comics who had logged thousands of hours of stage time.

Wright

You must have many people asking you to mentor them. How do you distinguish the farmers from the MBAs?

LaCroix

That is actually easier than you might think. I have what I call my "get the book" test. Many speakers want to learn to be funnier. When some of them hear my story, they come up to me after the program and ask me if I will help them. I tell a story of how the comedian I first approached recommended a certain book, *Stand-up Comedy, the Book,* by Judy Carter. I tell them if they want my help, the first thing they need to do is get the book. I never hear from ninety-nine percent of those people again.

For the one percent of those who do get back to me, the first question I ask is if they read the book. I refuse to answer any question until they read it. If they want my help, whether they are paying for my formal mentoring or asking only a few questions, why should I help them? If I give them a very simple task to go down the street and get a book—or even easier, buy it on-line—and they can't do that, they won't do anything else I tell them either. In my opinion, they are not true students and not committed to the process.

I very much believe in giving back, and I do. I give ten weekends a year to Toastmasters International and the National Speakers Association, and ten percent of my speaking income to charity, but my time is way too valuable to waste on someone not *committed to success.* Take a moment and look at it from the mentor's point of view. What do *we* want? We want eager students. We want people who will actually go out and do something with our suggestions.

Some weeks ago I was traveling to Chicago to speak, so I held one of my Humor Boot Camps. That week a man sent me an e-mail asking me if I would mentor him. He wanted to learn to be funnier. I told him about the Boot Camp. He said he would love to go but hated the traffic in the city, and it would mean a very long drive because he lived on the other side of the city. Long drive? What would you say? Look at it from my standpoint and my experience. Think of my five-hour drive to and from Portland, Maine, for five minutes of comedy stage time. What wouldn't I have done to spend a whole day with someone I wanted to sponge from? I was brutally honest with the man, and did not care if I upset him. *He did not get it.* He said he wanted to be successful, but I knew he had not really *decided* to make it happen. I held up a mirror for him and he finally got it. The day of Boot Camp he was the first one to arrive, and I was happy to spend extra time helping him. He had shifted to being a *farmer.* If he learned nothing else from me, that lesson alone will help him incredibly.

Wright

In your process you mentioned craving feedback. Why is that so important?

LaCroix

Kamikaze pilots! That's what I say.

I was watching the History Channel and got caught up in a special on Kamikaze pilots. If you can look objectively at this subject as a plan of war, without the emotional chaos behind it, it holds a powerful lesson. Say you are a Japanese commander and you can somehow convince your pilots to give up their lives in the name of their country, wouldn't that seem on the surface a pretty effective plan?

The television special stated that the Japanese commander's strategy was: one plane to take out one ship. Not a bad plan. Think of the devastation just one pilot could create. But the original plan did not work.

Do you know what the problem was? No feedback! The pilot was gone, so how could anyone report back on why the plan wasn't working? Here's what happened. As a Kamikaze pilot approached a ship, every gun on that ship aimed at that one plane. The ship was able to shoot down the plane before it even got close. Once this was realized, the plan was adjusted and the Japanese attacked with two and three planes. The strategy became much more successful.

My point is, no matter how good your original plans or strategy, you have to constantly be getting feedback to make it work. If you are not already successful in your target area, you must crave feedback to correct and adjust as you go.

I'm not a great writer. There was a point in my championship speech where all the audience members thought, "Wow, how did he know what I was thinking?" The reason I knew was that I'd practiced that speech in front of twenty-two live audiences before I gave it in the contest. Twenty-two audiences gave me feedback that taught me what they were thinking. That feedback was essential for me to revise the speech to get the reaction I was looking for.

I also noticed that when I asked previous World Champions for guidance, all of them felt feedback was important. They all craved it. To become the best, go to the best and learn from them. What do they think is important? Champions think differently from the average person. What is important to a new speaker is not the same as what is important to a World Champion. A new speaker might worry about which suit and tie to wear that day. A champion is focused on much more important questions, such as "how will each thing I do and say impact the thought process of the audience members?" I knew I had to adjust my thinking and start *thinking* like a champion in order to become one.

Most people are not confident enough to take the feedback. They all want "Mom feedback." They want to hear they are on the right track and that they won't have to adjust. Do you know why? Some of it is ego and some of it is not wanting to do the work. I went to Advanced Toastmaster clubs and said, "Look, my mother has already heard the speech (meaning I don't need a pat on the back), so please, rip me apart." They did. It was painful. Three times I was ready to quit. Three times I woke up the next morning with a better speech. If I could not stand up to an advanced club, how would I ever stand up to the twenty-one judges at the World Championship who were just waiting for me to screw up?

Whatever your goal is, crave feedback!

Wright

Do you have any closing thoughts on mastering success for our readers?

LaCroix

Definitely. People thought I was crazy trying to become a comedian. Do other people think your goal or passion is stupid? My friends thought I was stupid for driving five hours for five minutes of *stage time* with no pay. Now I get paid very well for a one-hour keynote speech, and I get to do what I love for a living. Now they consider me *lucky*. You can go from stupid to lucky. The people who think so missed seeing the hard work in the middle.

When I look at what I'm really getting paid for, it is not the hour on the platform today but the two-and-a-half hours on the road in the past. That commitment is what gave me mastery of the platform. It's what gave me the ability to change the way an audience thinks in just an hour. The result is value that clients are willing to pay for.

When you see people who are successful, instead of sitting back and thinking they are lucky, be proactive and ask them, "How did you do it?"

Take some serious time to answer these questions:

1. What is it, specifically, that you want to be successful at doing?
2. Who is the best at doing that?
3. How can you learn from them?
4. Can you develop a *farmer's attitude?*
5. Can you *decide* to be successful despite failures along the way?
6. Are you confident enough to be humble?
7. Can you crave feedback all the way?
8. When will you get started?

Deciding to get started is tough. I don't mean wanting to or saying you are going to. I mean truly *deciding*. I started stand-up comedy in 1992 and speaking professionally in 1994. As my career *slowly* grew I worked at a day job. I was a telemarketer for Bose Corporation®, and had to move back home with my parents because of my devastated finances. This is *not* something I'm proud of, but I'm comfortable telling the whole truth. I had a college degree from Bryant College (now Bryant University), yet I remained at an entry-level position. People thought I was crazy (apparently this is normal in my life, and not uncommon among successful people). I could easily have moved up the corporate ladder. I chose not to.

I looked at things differently. Had I moved up I would have lost the flexibility my current job offered to change my schedule at the drop of a hat and accommodate a last-minute speaking engagement. I had the "safety net" of my Bose paycheck and benefits, and I could still pursue my dream. I kept telling people every year for five years that I was going to quit my day job in January and start speaking full-time.

August 25, 2001, I had worked hard enough to win Toastmasters International World Championship of Public Speaking. Just two weeks later we all experienced the wake-up call of September 11. Still that wasn't enough to get me to leave my day job. One month later, Dave McIlhenny, one of my two speaker coaches who helped me win the competition, unexpectedly passed away. OUCH! Brad, a co-worker and fellow Toastmaster, pulled me aside and asked me when I was going to finally leave Bose and venture out on my own. I told him "I can't. I don't have enough speaking engagements lined up to leave my safety net." He looked at me and said softly, "Darren, you've been saying that for years. Bose isn't your safety net, it's your *dragnet.*" I stood there speechless. Wow—right between the eyes. How do you argue with that?

I looked at my life and thought if I don't do it now, when would I ever make the leap? It took me time to swallow that. Once I did, I *decided.* I walked in the next morning and gave one day's notice. I had great friends who asked what they could do to help. I replied, "Save me a place at the dinner table, I might not be able to afford to eat." I was serious.

I had heard (though I cannot confirm) that Bill Cosby started out performing at colleges for free and sold his cassette tapes in the back of the room. I had just come out with my book, *Laugh & Get Rich.* I figured I could go speak for free and offer my books for sale in the back of the room. If I could sell just a few books a day I could replace my Bose income and spend the rest of the time marketing myself. I committed a year to myself and never looked back.

I don't suggest everyone quit their day job without laying some groundwork first. You still have to be smart about it. I did not have a family to support and I learned to live on next to nothing, but you have to ask yourself: *what is your dragnet?*

I've had the privilege of speaking around the world, especially to fellow Toastmasters. I always run into people who are jealous of my winning the World Championship of Public Speaking. I understand that, but I like to remind them that I've never run into *anyone* who is jealous of the work it took me to get there. *That* is what they *should* be jealous of.

Wright

What a great conversation. I really appreciate all the time you have taken with us today, Darren. I know our readers will learn a lot, as I have. Today we have been talking with Darren LaCroix, who by his own admission was not funny when he started but became a professional comedian. Not only that, he took his story all the way to the World Championship of Public Speaking, and out of 25,000 contestants from fourteen countries he was crowned the 2001 World Champion of Public Speaking.

Darren, thank you so much for being with us and sharing all this with us today on *Masters of Success.*

About The Author

Darren LaCroix, the World Champion of Public Speaking, is in demand as a motivational keynote speaker and has inspired audiences as far away as Singapore, Malaysia, and Taiwan. He coaches CEOs in presentation skills and has created numerous educational programs, including *Speak Like a Champion* and *Learn How the Pros Make 'em Laugh.* Translated into three languages, his first book, *Laugh & Get Rich,* is in its fourth printing. *Just for Laffs* is his comedy DVD.

Darren LaCroix

The Humor Institute, Inc.

Phone: 888.528.4451

www.DarrenLaCroix.com

www.Humor411.com

For Darren's free e-newsletter:

www.Presentation411.com

Chapter Ten

JACK CANFIELD

THE INTERVIEW

David E. Wright (Wright)

Today we are talking with Jack Canfield. You probably know him as the founder and co-creator of the *New York Times* number one best-selling *Chicken Soup for the Soul* book series, which currently has thirty-five titles and seventy-eight million copies in print in over thirty-two languages. Jack's background includes a Batchelor's from Harvard, a Master's from the University of Massachusetts and an Honorary Doctorate from the University of Santa Monica. He has been a high school and university teacher, a workshop facilitator, a psychotherapist, and for the past twenty-five years, a leading authority in the area of self-esteem and personal development.

Jack Canfield, welcome to *Masters of Success!*

Jack Canfield (Canfield)

Thank you David. It's great to be with you.

Wright

I talked with Mark Victor Hansen a few days ago. He gave you full credit for coming up with the idea of the *Chicken Soup* series. Obviously it's made you an internationally known personality. Other than recognition, has the series changed you personally and if so, how?

Canfield

I would say that it has and I think it has in a couple of ways. Number one, I read stories all day long of people who've overcome what would feel like insurmountable obstacles. For example we just did a book *Chicken Soup for the Unsinkable Soul.* There's a story in there about a single mother with three daughters. She got a disease and had to have both of her hands and both of her feet amputated. She got prosthetic devices and was able to learn how to use them so she could cook, drive the car, brush her daughters' hair, get a job, etc. I read that and I think, "God, what would I ever have to complain and whine and moan about?" So I think at one level it's just given me a great sense of gratitude and appreciation for everything I have and has made me less irritable about the little things.

I think the other thing that's happened for me personally is my sphere of influence has changed. By that I mean, for example, a couple of years ago I was asked to be keynote speaker for the Women's Congressional Caucus. The Caucus includes women in Congress, Senators, Governors, and Lieutenant Governors in America.

I asked, "What do you want me to talk about—what topic?"

"Whatever you think we need to know to be better legislators," was the reply.

And I thought, "Wow! They want *me* to tell *them* about what laws they should be making and what would make a better culture?"

Well, that wouldn't have happened if our books hadn't come out and I hadn't become famous. I think I get to play with people at a higher level and have more influence in the world. That's important to me because my life purpose is inspiring and empowering people to live their highest vision so the world works for everybody. I get to do that on a much bigger level than when I was just a high school teacher back in Chicago.

Wright

I think one of the powerful components of that book series is that you can read a positive story in just a few minutes. You can also come back and revisit it. I know my daughter, who is thirteen now, has three of the books and she just reads them interchangeably. Sometimes I go in her bedroom and she'll be crying and reading one of them. Other times she'll be laughing, so they really are chicken soup for the soul, aren't they?

Canfield

They really are. In fact we have four books in the *Teenage Soul* series now and a new one coming out at the end of this year. We have a new book called *Chicken Soup for the Teenage Soul and the Tough Stuff.* It's all about dealing with parents' divorces, teachers who don't understand you, boyfriends who drink and drive, and subjects like that.

I have a son who's eleven and he has a twelve-year-old friend (a girl). I asked my son's friend, "Why do you like this book?"

She said, "You know, whenever I'm feeling down I read it; it makes me cry and I feel better. Some of the stories make me laugh and some of the stories make me feel more responsible for my life. But basically I just feel like I'm not alone."

One of the people I work with recently said that the books are like a support group between the covers of a book. People can read about others' experiences and realize they're not the only one going through something.

Wright

Jack, with our *Masters of Success* publication we're trying to encourage people in our audience to be better, to live better, and be more fulfilled by listening to the examples of our guests. Is there anything or anyone in your life who has made a difference for you and helped you to become a better person?

Canfield

Yes and we could do ten shows just on that. I'm influenced by people all the time. If I were to go way back I'd have to say one of the key influences in my life was Jesse Jackson when he was still a minister in Chicago. I was teaching in an all black high school there and I went to Jesse Jackson's church with a friend one time. What happened for me was I saw somebody with a vision. (This was before Martin Luther King was killed and Jesse was of the lieutenants in his organization.) I just saw people trying to make the world work better for a certain segment of the population. I was inspired by that kind of visionary belief—that it's possible to make change.

Then later John F. Kennedy was a hero of mine. I was very much inspired by him.

Robert Resnick is a therapist I had for two years and he was an inspiration for me. He taught me a little formula called E + R = O. That stands for Events plus Response equals Outcome. He said, "If you don't like your outcomes quit blaming the events and start changing your responses." One of his favorite phrases was, "If the grass on the other side of the fence looks greener, start watering your own lawn more."

I think it helped me get off from any kind of self-pity I might have had because I had parents who were alcoholics. It's very easy to blame them for my life not working. They weren't very successful or rich and I was surrounded by people who were. I felt like, "God, what if I'd had parents like they had? I could have been a lot better." He just got me off that whole notion and made me realize the hand I was dealt is the hand I've got to play, take responsibility for who I am, quit complaining and blaming others, and get on with my life. That was a turning point for me.

I'd say the last person who really affected me big-time was a guy named W. Clement Stone who was a self-made multi-millionaire in Chicago. He taught me that success is not a four-letter word, it's nothing to be ashamed of and you ought to go for it. He said, "The best thing you can do for the poor is not be one of them." Be a model for what it is to live a successful life. So I learned the principles of success from him and that's what I've been teaching now for the last almost thirty years.

Wright

He was the entrepreneur in the insurance industry, wasn't he?

Canfield

He was. He had combined insurance and when I worked for him he was worth six hundred million dollars. That was before the dot.com millionaires came along in Silicon Valley. He just knew more about success. He was a good friend of Napoleon Hill, the man who wrote *Think and Grow Rich*. He was a fabulous mentor. I really learned a lot from him.

Wright

I miss some of the men I listened to when I was a young salesman coming up and he was one of them. Napoleon Hill was another one and Dr. Peale—all of their writings made me who I am today. I'm glad I had that opportunity.

Canfield

One speaker whose name you probably will remember is Charlie "Tremendous" Jones. He says, "Who we are is a result of the books we read and the people we hang out with." I think that's so true and that's why I tell people, "If you want to have high self-esteem, hang out with people with high self-esteem. If you want to be more spiritual hang out with spiritual people." We're always telling our children, "Don't hang out with those kids." The reason we don't want them to associate with certain kinds of people is we know how influential people are with each other. I think we need to give ourselves the same advice. Who are we hanging out with? We can hang out with them in cassette tapes, CDs, books like yours, and in person.

Wright

One of my favorites was a fellow named Bill Gove from Florida. I talked with him about three or four years ago; he's retired now. His mind is still as quick as it ever was. I thought he was one of the greatest speakers I had ever heard.

What do you think makes up a great mentor? In other words, are there characteristics that mentors seem to have in common?

Canfield

I think there are three obvious ones. One is I think they have to have the time to do it and two is the willingness to do it. I also think they need to be someone who is doing something you want to do.

W. Clement Stone used to tell me, "If you want to be rich hang out with rich people. Watch what they do, eat what they eat, dress the way they dress—try it on." He wasn't suggesting that I give up my authentic self, but he was pointing out that they probably have habits I didn't have. His advice was to study them and study the people who are already like you. I always ask salespeople in an organization, "Who are the top two or three in your organization?" I tell them to start taking them out to lunch and dinner and for a drink and finding out what they do. Ask them, "What's your secret?" Nine times out of ten they'll be willing to tell you.

It goes back to what we said earlier about asking. I'll go into corporations and I'll say, "Who are the top ten people?"

They'll tell me and I'll say, "Did you ever ask them what they do that is different than what you do?"

They'll reply, "No."

"Why not?"

"Well they might not want to tell me."

"How do you know? Did you ever ask them? The worst thing they can do is say no. You'll be no worse off than you are now."

So I think with mentors you just look at people who seem to be living the life you want to live and achieving the results you want to achieve. And then what we tell them in our book is, when you approach a mentor they're probably busy and successful and so they haven't got a lot of time. Just ask, "Can I talk to you for ten minutes every month?" If I know it's only going to be ten minutes I'll probably say yes. The neat thing is if I like you I'll always give you more than ten minutes, but that ten minutes gets me in the door.

Wright

In the future are there any more Jack Canfield books authored singularly?

Canfield

Yes, I'm working on two books right now. One is called $E + R = O$, which is that little formula I told you about earlier. I just feel I want to get that out there because every time I give a speech and talk about that the whole room gets so quiet you can hear a pin drop. I can tell that people are really getting value.

Then I'm going to do a series of books on the principles of success. I've got about 150 of them that I've identified over the years. I have a book down the road I want to do that's called *No More Put-Downs* which is a book probably aimed mostly at parents, teachers, and managers. There's a culture we have now of put-down humor whether it's *Married With Children* or *All in the Family*—there's that characteristic of macho put-down humor. There's research now that's showing how bad it is for kids' self-esteem, and for coworkers and for athletes (when the coaches do it) so I want to get that message out there as well.

Wright

It's really not that funny, is it?

Canfield

No. We'll laugh it off because we don't want to look like we're a wimp but underneath we're hurt. The research now shows that you're better off breaking a child's bones than you are breaking their spirit. A bone will heal much more quickly than their emotional spirit will.

Wright

I remember recently reading a survey where people listed the top five people who had influenced them in their lives. I've tried it on a couple of groups at church and other places. In my case (and in the survey that's running) I found that about three out of people's top five mentors are always teachers. I wonder if that's going to be the same in the next decade.

Canfield

I think that's probably because as children we're in our most formative years. We actually spend more time with our teachers than we do with our parents. Research shows that the average parent only interacts verbally with each of their children only about eight and a half minutes a day. Yet at school you're interacting with your teacher for anywhere from six to eight hours, depending on how long the school day is. This includes interaction with coaches, chorus directors, etc.

I think that in almost everybody's life there's been that one teacher who loved them as a human being, not just as a student—some person they were supposed to fill full of history and English—and that person believed in them and inspired them.

Les Brown is one of the great motivational speakers in the world. If it hadn't been for one teacher who said, "I think you can do more than be in a special ed. class; I think you're the one," he'd probably still be cutting grass in the median strip of the highways in Florida instead of a successful presenter who can receive $35,000 as a keynote speaker.

Wright

I had a conversation one time with Les when he was talking about this wonderful teacher who discovered he was dyslexic. Everybody else called him dumb but this one lady took him under her wing and had him tested. His entire life changed because of her interest in him.

Canfield

I'm on the board of advisors of the Dyslexic Awareness Resource Center here in Santa Barbara. The reason is because I taught at a high school with a lot of kids who were considered "at-risk." They were kids who would end up in gangs and so forth.

What we found over and over was that about seventy-eight percent of all the kids in the juvenile detention centers in Chicago were kids who had learning disabilities—primarily dyslexia—but there were others as well. They were never diagnosed and they weren't doing well in school so they'd drop out. As soon as you drop out of school you become subject to the influence of gangs and other kinds of criminal and drug linked activities.

If these kids had just been diagnosed earlier, we'd have probably gotten rid of half of the juvenile crime in America because there are a lot of really good programs that can teach dyslexics to read and so forth.

Wright

My wife is a teacher and she brings home stories that are heart-breaking about parents not being as concerned about their children as they used to be or not as helpful as they used to be. Did you find that to be a problem when you were teaching?

Canfield

It depends on what kind of district you're in. If it's a poor district the parents could be drugged out, on alcohol, and basically just not available. If you're in a really high rent district the parents are not available because they're both working and coming home tired, or they're jet-setters, or they're working late at the office because they're workaholics. Sometimes it really takes two paychecks to pay the rent anymore. I find that the majority of parents care but often they don't know what to do. They don't know how to discipline their children. They don't know how to help them with their homework. They're not passing on skills because they themselves never got them. Unfortunately the trend tends to be like a chain letter. The people with the least amount of skills tend to have the most number of children. The other thing is you get "crack babies" [addiction to crack cocaine was passed through the mother's bloodstream]. In Los Angeles one out of every ten babies born is a crack baby.

Wright

That's unbelievable.

Canfield

Yes and another statistic shows that by the time they're twelve years old, fifty percent of the kids in the U.S. have started experimenting with alcohol. I see a lot of that in the Bible belt. You don't see the big city, urban designer drugs; but there is a lot of alcoholism.

Another thing you get, unfortunately, is a lot of familial violence—a lot of kids getting beat up and hit, parents who drink and then explode; and, as we talked about earlier, child abuse and sexual abuse—you see a lot of that.

Wright

Most people are fascinated by these television shows about being a survivor. What has been the greatest comeback from adversity that you have made in your career or in your life?

Canfield

You know it's funny, I don't think I've had a lot of major failures and setbacks where I had to start over. My life's been kind of on an intentional curve. But I do have a lot of challenges. Mark and I are always setting goals that challenge us. We always say, "The purpose of setting a really big goal is not so that you can achieve it so much, but it's who you become in the process of achieving it."

A friend of mine, Jim Rose, says, "You want to set goals big enough so that in the process of achieving them you become someone worth being."

I think that to be a millionaire is nice but so what? People make the money and then they lose it. People get the big houses and they burn down or Silicon Valley goes belly up and all of a sudden they don't have a big house anymore. But whom you became in the process of learning how to do that can never be taken away from you.

What we do is we constantly put big challenges in front of us. Right now we have a new book called *Chicken Soup for the Teacher's Soul.* (You'll have to make sure to get a copy for your wife.) I was a teacher and I was a teacher trainer for years. But in the last seven years, because of the success of the *Chicken Soup* books, I haven't been in the education world that much. I've got to go out and relearn how I market to that world.

I met with a Superintendent of Schools. I met with a guy named Jason Dorsey who's one of the number one consultants in the world in that area. I found out who has the best-selling book in that area. I sat down with his wife for a day and talked about her marketing approaches.

So I believe that if you face any kind of adversity, whether it's losing your job, death of a spouse, divorce, an accident like Christopher Reeves where you become paralyzed, or whatever, you simply do what you have to do. You find people who have already handled the situation and look at how they got through it. You find out either from their books, or from their tapes, or by talking with them, or interviewing them, and you get the support you need to get through it. Whether it's a counselor in your church, or you go on a retreat, or you read the Bible, do something that will give you the support you need to get to the other end.

You also have to know what the end you want is. Do you want to be remarried? Do you just want to have a job and be a single mom? What is it? You need to reach out and ask for support; I think people really like to help other people. They're not always available because sometimes they're going through it themselves, but there's always someone with a helping hand. Often I think we let our pride get in the way. We let our stubbornness get in the way. We let our belief in how the world should be get in our way instead of dealing with how the world *is*. When we get that out of the way then we can start doing that which we need to do to get where we need to go.

Wright

If you could have a platform and tell our audience something you feel that would help or encourage them, what would you say?

Canfield

I'd say number one, believe in yourself, believe in your dreams, and trust your feelings. I think too many people are trained wrong when they're little kids. For instance, they're mad at their daddy and they're told, "You're not mad at your Daddy."

They say, "Gee, I thought I was."

Or you say, "That's going to hurt."

The doctor says, "No it's not." Then he or she gives you the shot and it hurts.

The doctor says, "See, that didn't hurt, did it?"

The result is you start not to trust yourself.

Or you ask your mom, "Are you upset?"

Your mom says, "No," but she really is. So you stop learning to trust your perception.

I tell the story over and over there are hundreds of people I've met who've come from upper class families where they make big incomes and the dad's a doctor, and the kid wants to be a mechanic and work in an auto shop because that's what he loves. The family says, "That's beneath us. You can't do that." So the kid ends up being an anesthesiologist killing three people because he's not paying attention. What he really wants to do is tinker with cars.

I tell people you've got to trust your own feelings—your own motivations, what turns you on, what you want to do, what makes you feel good—and quit worrying about what other people say, think, or want for you. Decide what you want for yourself and then do what you need to do to go about getting it. It takes work.

I always tell people that I read a book a week minimum and at the end of the year I've read fifty-two books. We're talking about professional books, books on self-help, finances, psychology, parenting, and so forth. At the end of ten years you've read 520 books. That puts me in the top one percent of people knowing stuff in this country. But most people are spending their time watching television.

W. Clement Stone told me when I went to work for him, "I want you to cut out one hour a day of television."

"Okay, what do I do with it?" I asked him.

He said, "Read."

He told me what kind of materials to read. He said, "At the end of a year you'll have spent 365 hours reading. Divide that by a forty-hour work week and that's nine and a half weeks of education every year."

I thought, "Wow! That's two months." It's like going back to summer school. As a result of that I have close to 8,000 books in my library.

The reason I'm on your show instead of someone else's is that people like Jim Rohn, Les Brown, you, and I read a lot. We listen to tapes and we go to those seminars. That's why we're the people with the information. I always say that your raise becomes effective when you do. You'll become more effective as you gain more skills, more insight, and more knowledge.

Wright

Jack, I have watched your career for over a decade and your accomplishments are just outstanding. But your humanitarian efforts are really what impress me. I think that you're doing great things, not only in California, but all over the country as well.

Canfield

It's true. In addition to all of the work we do, we pick one to three charities. We've given away over six million dollars in the last eight years, along with our publisher who matches every penny we give away. We've planted over a million trees in Yosemite National Park. We've paid for hundreds of thousands of cataract operations in third world countries. We've contributed to the Red Cross, the Humane Society, and on it goes. It feels like a real blessing to be able to make that kind of a contribution in the world.

Wright

Today we have been talking with Jack Canfield, founder and co-creator of the *Chicken Soup for the Soul* book series, which currently has thirty-five titles and I'll have to update this. It was fifty-three million. How many has it been now, Jack?

Canfield

We're almost up to seventy-eight million. We have a new book titled *Chicken Soup for the Soul of America*. It contains stories that grew out of 9/11—it's a real healing book for our nation. I would encourage your listeners to get a copy and share it with their families.

Wright

I will stand in line to get one of those. Thank you so much for being with us today.

About Jack Canfield

Jack Canfield is one of America's leading experts on developing self-esteem and peak performance. A dynamic and entertaining speaker, as well as a highly sought-after trainer, he has a wonderful ability to inform and inspire audiences toward developing their own human potential and personal effectiveness. Jack Canfield is most well known for the *Chicken Soup for the Soul* series, which he co-authored with Mark Victor Hansen, and for his audio programs about building high self-esteem. Jack is the founder of Self-Esteem Seminars, located in Santa Barbara, California. The seminars train entrepreneurs, educators, corporate leaders, and employees how to accelerate the achievement of their personal and professional goals. Jack is also founder of The Foundation for Self Esteem, located in Culver City, California, which provides self-esteem resources and training to social workers, welfare recipients, and human resource professionals. Jack graduated from Harvard in 1966, received his M.E. degree at the university of Massachusetts in 1973, and an Honorary Doctorate from the University of Santa Monica. He has been a high school and university teacher, a workshop facilitator, a psychotherapist, and for the past thirty years, a leading authority in the area of self-esteem and personal development. As a result of his work with prisoners, welfare recipients, and inner-city youth, Jack was appointed by the state legislature to the California Task Force to Promote Self-Esteem and Personal and Social Responsibility. He also served on the board of trustees of the National Council for Self-Esteem.

Jack Canfield

P.O. Box 30880

Santa Barbara, CA 93130

Email: info4jack@jackcanfield.com

Chapter Eleven

DENISE LANDERS

David Wright (Wright)

Today we are talking with Denise Landers. Denise is a productivity trainer and an organizing specialist. As the owner of Key Organization Systems Inc., she works with businesses and individuals to develop systems for improved workflow. Denise is a featured speaker for business meetings and conferences and her clients include the Internal Revenue Service, University of Texas and M.D. Anderson Cancer Center, all of which have booked her training seminars and consulting services for their staffs. Her company has been featured on television as one of the small companies contributing to our nation's productivity.

Denise, welcome to *Masters of Success*.

Denise Landers (Landers)

Thank you, David.

Wright

Let's talk about some of the things you do. Time management systems and training have been hot topics for many years. What makes your work different?

Landers

David, the difference we bring to becoming more effective time managers is that we provide a very concrete process that can be immediately implemented, and we can stay to develop it with clients. We often hear from prospects, "When I have time, I'm going to do this." Instead, when we come in, the office management has actually made a commitment to get organized. We see the full process put into place at that time as opposed to those who want to get organized but put it on the back burner waiting for those free hours that never materialize.

Wright

What immediate benefits result when you have worked in an office developing these processes?

Landers

The words we hear used so often by executives and business owners include: "exhilaration," "a feeling of freedom," and, "a sense of control." In just one day with our *8-Hour Miracle®*, we are changing not only the physical look of the space but also the mental outlook of our clients. We had one client with a national remodeling business who asked if we told people how light and free they feel when we're done. The reduction of stress is incredible!

Wright

On the bottom line, it's all about the customers and clients. How does that affect the perceptions of the business's customer or client?

Landers

When customers or clients come into an office and sees a clear, organized space as opposed to stacks and chaos, they have so much more confidence in the business's ability to handle their needs. A photo example I often show is a financial planner's office in which I worked. When you walked into that office, you saw stacks of unopened monthly statements all over and piles of papers on all available surfaces. Do you think you would have confidence that this person is handling your retirement funds in a competent way? That is what I mean by the look of the office. What impression do you get?

Attorneys are another example. Many people have never been in their attorney's office. Their meetings are in a conference room, and the appearance of the offices is often the reason! There may not be space for the clients to sit. The clients wouldn't feel they were getting the attention for which they were paying if they saw case files strewn around.

Wright

I understand that there are also physical long-term effects that can result from putting organized systems into place. What would some of these be?

Landers

We are now in a society where most of us have far too much to do and too little time in which to do it. Stress is a natural result of this. We have all become aware of the problems associated with stress. It can lead to illness, absenteeism, and loss of productivity. In addition, stress on just one person in an office can lead to stress on all those around, as colleagues are required to take on more responsibilities because of stress-related absenteeism. Within the office the colleagues may have to deal with the moods and the attitudes caused by this pressure.

There's a growing body of scientific research showing that multi-tasking can make you less efficient. We joke about "senior moments" but those brief lapses are actually becoming a reality. This is something we have done to ourselves, damaging our brain cells with the constant firing in multiple directions. We are physically hurting ourselves. When we try to do two or three things at once in quick succession, we are taking much longer to accomplish them than we would if we did them one at a time. With multi-tasking we have reduced the brainpower available for each task and have created the possibility of short-term memory loss.

Wright

Before we go on, you didn't pay a private detective to check out my office, did you?

Landers

You're not unique in that area. We are all burdened with challenges in keeping our time and space in order. It's that problem of too much to do and too little time in which to do it.

Wright

I think you have actually seen my office!

How prevalent today is disorganization within the business world, and what does this cost us?

Landers

Statistics show that the average businessperson is wasting over one hour per day. That's one hour per day, per employee in an organization, multiplied by years of this, and that's a really conservative amount. If a person stopped for just one day to get organized, he would gain all that time back and in less than two weeks would be working ahead for the remainder of the year. Consider that it is also not just people who are totally disorganized. We might be called in by the person whom everyone else thinks is organized. That person who is somewhat organized, however, knows that he could be much more productive if he added to his work systems.

Often people do not stop to see the solution because they are in the middle of the situation. Sometimes it takes an outside person to come in and ask, "Why are you doing it this way? Have you considered looking at this in another way?" Many times it is because they have always done it a certain way. We encourage them to change their perspectives.

Wright

Why would people procrastinate on making changes when they know that their current methods of operation are not working as efficiently as possible?

Landers

People do procrastinate on making changes even when they know that they are not working as efficiently as possible and they are frustrated by their inability to get more things done. The number one reason for this procrastination is that they feel they don't have time to stop what they are doing in order to become better organized. They actually become like the little boy lost in the woods. The deeper into the woods he goes, the faster he runs. There are so many deadlines to meet and so many daily crises. These people are not willing to commit the time to get organized right now. Yet, they would meet these deadlines and avoid many crises if they were organized...it becomes a vicious cycle.

Wright

What is the solution to the inability to find time?

Landers

People really do want to become better organized and more productive. Disorganization negatively impacts their work, as well as others' perceptions of them, so instead of saying, "As soon as I have time..." they will have to write it into their schedules. There is no other way except putting it on their calendars. They might decide to work for one hour every Friday afternoon, or they might choose to work on Saturday. Whatever they decide, it must be written into their schedules.

Wright

Let's get down to the money part. What are the financial ramifications of allowing disorganization to continue in the workplace?

Landers

We all know that the expenditure of money is always a consideration for companies, especially in this time when businesses are struggling to recover from the setbacks of the past few years. A company may hire administrative assistants and then think it is the job of these individuals to get them organized. Yet consider that the ones doing the hiring are the ones with all of the degrees and certifications, and they haven't been able to get themselves organized. I frequently hear from people that they hired an assistant to get them organized and he or she didn't do it. My response to that is, "You are the one with the degrees and certifications. If you can't do this for yourself, then why do you think you can hire somebody at a lower pay level and a lower skill level and think they are going to do it for you?" The reality is that a lot of these new hires are very capable of maintaining and even tweaking processes but most find it beyond their skill level to develop a full procedure for the office.

When we are thinking about financial ramifications, we need to calculate the number of hours wasted each day and then translate that into a dollar figure by multiplying the number of days in a year times the number of employees to which this is happening times the number of years that this situation has continued. Is it really more efficient for an assistant to struggle over a year or two trying to create a sensible system or to have the full department operating at peak efficiently within days?

Wright

How do you implement this training within a company or department?

Landers

When we are working with a department to develop better organization, we often start with a morning seminar for the entire group. Our initial session may begin by presenting a process that allows for handling all the incoming activities of the day, which can include paper, e-mails, voice mail, and verbal requests. We take all of these and put them into a system that easily prioritizes and focuses on one task at a time, eliminating some of that multi-tasking we talked about earlier. After our training session, everyone goes back to the office and actually begins to put the processes for daily workflow into place. My staff and I circulate so that we spend time with each individual involved until all have implemented this process, modifying it to match each job within the department or company.

Wright

What is the biggest advantage in training a company or a department together?

Landers

The advantage of focusing on the whole department is that everyone is on the same page, so to speak. This provides accountability within a department. In most organizations now, if one staff member had something unfortunate happen and was away from work for two weeks or a month without prior notice, no one would have a clue what their work plans would be for that first day and the upcoming days. When you have a departmental system, you can cover the most immediate concerns or hire a temporary replacement without a major setback.

Wright

How does group training differ from working with an individual?

Landers

Sometimes, rather than working with the whole department or company, we are hired by one individual within a company to work with him or her alone. When we work with single business owners, home offices, or individuals within a department we literally start with the first piece of paper before us on the desk, we determine the next step, and we establish a location for that activity. The two questions we use in looking at items are, "What is your next step?" and "When do you have a reasonable chance of completing it?" Since we are not focusing on group interaction and understanding of the system, we teach the system as we implement it.

Wright

Besides setting up processes for incoming work, what do you emphasize at this stage?

Landers

The training we provide also includes techniques for effective scheduling. We are four times more effective if we can work on one type of activity at a time. When we multi-task, we rapidly switch back and forth between things, such as juggling telephone calls with emails and quick verbal responses. It actually takes much longer to do this switching than handling all of your phone calls at one time and then switching over to deal with your e-mails. Our training includes setting-up blocks of time each day so that we can limit our multi-tasking and actually get more done as a result.

Wright

Isn't one of the biggest complaints within companies that they cannot get work done because of all of the interruptions that occur?

Landers

This is a major problem cited by most of the companies with which I have worked. It's definitely aggravated by conditions in many work places today where everyone is required to take on more tasks as outgoing staff is replaced. The situation becomes like that of the frog in the pot of hot water. When you put a frog in a pot of boiling water, he will immediately jump out. When the heat is turned up little by little, however, the frog gets boiled without knowing it. This is similar to many of today's workplaces. As more responsibilities are added, piece by piece we become overwhelmed without realizing what has happened.

Included in the processes we teach are techniques for handling telephone calls, e-mails, and visitors. Other interruptions within an office can relate to the layout of the space, so we take that into consideration when setting up an effective workspace. Since people also constantly interrupt themselves, we create an awareness of this. While we will never be able to completely do away with interruptions, eighty percent of those interruptions can be eliminated and the other twenty percent can be shortened and controlled.

Wright

What about e-mail? It seems to be developing into a huge time consuming issue for people in business.

Landers

E-mail has become such an important topic that we now address it with specific seminars. We talk about how to write an effective e-mail designed to limit return e-mail, how to use the functions of software programs, how to keep inboxes clear, how to keep tasks prioritized within e-mail, and how to more rapidly read onscreen. We normally read thirty to fifty percent slower when reading directly from the screen, and learning speed-reading techniques relative to the computer screen can be a big time-saver.

Wright

What can a client expect after working with you for one or two days?

Landers

At the end of our sessions, whether with one individual or the individuals within a company or department, each desk area is cleared, there are no piles around the desk, and usually a new filing system has been implemented. Keep in mind, however, that our goal is not the elimination of the piles but the development of the system. The physical clean-up is a nice result of the new organization, but it is not what we are striving for. We are not about all your pens being lined up in a row or pretty little labels on everything. We are about working as effectively and efficiently as possible.

Wright

What are some of the problems with the common ways of filing today?

Landers

The main problem today is that we are still filing the way we did hundreds of years ago, using the alphabetical system, and it no longer works. For example, if we take a simple piece of paper such as the car insurance, how do we file it? It could fit under "car," "auto," "insurance," "State Farm," "Ford," or "vehicle." So we pick one of these titles, and three months later we can't remember how we labeled it, so we make a new file. Then our spouse comes in and tries to find that paper, and he or she is thinking "auto" while we put it under "State Farm." In an office, multiply that by the number of people filing and retrieving papers, and calculate how many times a day such a thing happens. Rarely today does someone pick up a piece of paper and think of just one word. Yet we are trying to cram one or two thoughts onto a tab, and since we know we probably won't be able to find it later, we often don't file it at all.

I like to use a numbered system based on keywords. It involves software that locates the paper for you. This equates to using Google for your file cabinets, allowing you to keep your papers in paper form, without scanning, while the computer finds them for you.

Wright

I'm in real trouble. I would have probably filed it under "P" for paper.

Landers

You might, but who else would know that? Even if you remembered it later, your assistant and your colleagues wouldn't find it, and that's where the problems lie.

Wright

What advice would you offer to business owners and managers who are focused on increasing their productivity?

Landers

If there are pockets of disorganization, don't avoid them or walk around them, no matter who is involved. Even one disorganized person in a group affects all the others. That person may not have his part of the project done, or he may constantly interrupt others, asking for information that's buried on his own desk. The very small cost of becoming organized pays big dividends within days. Most businesses are doing more work with fewer resources, and by maximizing their available resources they are increasing productivity while at the same time minimizing stress in the work place.

Wright

Well I have learned a lot here today. I'm going to go right back to the office and start some new processes before you come down and inspect me.

Landers

Put it on your calendar, David. Make sure that organizing time is scheduled.

Wright

I want you to know that I really appreciate the time you have spent with me. This is really an important issue, and I was just sitting here thinking that I have only about fourteen employees, but if I calculate that dollar amount, I don't even want to consider what disorganization has cost over the last five years.

Landers

Absolutely! You have to think about that as well as the stress created in trying to work through all the inefficiencies.

Wright

Today we have been talking with Denise Landers, a productivity trainer and organizing specialist. Her company works with businesses and individuals helping to create easy-to-use processes for dealing with the overwhelming workloads and multi-tasking requirements that most businesses face today, from the CEO to the administrative assistants.

About The Author

Denise Landers is the owner of Key Organization Systems, Inc. As a productivity trainer and organizing specialist, she helps companies, educational institutions, and individuals design tailored systems for efficient workflow. Having seen and experienced the time management challenges confronting us in a fast-faced and demanding workplace, her company focuses on providing the skills that are needed to increase efficiency while coping with the multiple demands on our time.

Denise Landers

Phone: 281.397.0015

Email: dlanders@keyorganization.com

www.keyorganization.com

Chapter Twelve

DARLENE T. CARVER

David E. Wright (Wright)

Today we're talking with Darlene T. Carver. Darlene is founder and "Queen Bee" of Merlin & Associates, Inc., a training and consulting firm. Darlene's entire life has been devoted to helping others succeed. She does this through her instruction as a seminar leader, speaker, and consultant for people in academia, industry, and government. She inspires people to acquire strong communication and problem-solving skills, work effectively on teams, expand strategies to cope with demands through time and stress management techniques, and to develop essential managerial skills. Darlene also works with the United States Army as a counselor assisting military and civilians who are making career transitions.

Darlene, welcome to *Masters of Success*.

Carver

Thank you, David.

Wright

So what do you think makes for a successful person?

Carver

Well, success can be defined by many standards. I am successful when I know I have impacted someone else in a positive way. For example, when I have someone in my workshop who gets one of those "Ah ha!" moments, I know that I have been successful. Success is also a strong determination and a drive that possesses someone to move in a successful direction so that he or she can accomplish what he or she wants. Leo F. Buscaglia, teacher, writer, and humanitarian, has said:

"It's not enough to have lived. We should be determined to live for something. May I suggest that it be creating joy for others, sharing what we have for the betterment of personkind, bringing hope to the lost and love to the lonely."

I don't believe that success is necessarily fame, wealth, or power, although I know a lot of people do define success that way. Many people tend to define success in tangible items, such as owning a bigger house or a more expensive car. These things make them feel they have "arrived"—are successful. And I agree that these things do give us a feeling of success, but it's not the deep felt success that makes a person truly successful—it's only superficial.

For someone to be truly successful, he or she should look at success in a holistic way. Stephen R. Covey, author of *The 7 Habits of Highly Effective People,* did a good job of describing this concept in his four dimensions of life: to live, to love, to learn, and to leave a legacy. I interpret his dimensions this way:

- *To live*—To think of each day as a new blank page and to give it your fullest attention because it just might be your last.
- *To love*—To have family and friends whom you cherish like a support group you know you can turn to when you need them.
- *To learn*—Expand your horizons every day by exploring something you did not know. I tell my seminar participants that I will learn as much from them as they will learn from me because I believe it's a mutual learning environment.
- *To leave a legacy*—This is really the most visible and tangible concept for me. I founded a private, postsecondary business school that is my legacy to the community. The fact that it has continued and succeeded with different owners for more than twenty-five years gives me great pride. To see my graduates from all walks of life pursing their dreams and becoming successful in their own right gives me a true sense of fulfillment. The school even has second and third gen-

fulfillment. The school even has second and third generation students and to me that's really exciting.

I believe someone is successful when they consistently seek to help others—always searching for opportunities, large or small.

Wright

So how have you applied that to your own life?

Carver

Because of my profession—speaking, training, and consulting—I feel blessed that the opportunity to impact others occurs daily for me. It is my personal mission. As my mission statement says, "To make a difference in the lives of others, both human and animal, by using my knowledge, skills, and abilities to help them succeed." (I put in the animal reference because I am also very involved with animals and have a great love for them.)

When people work in jobs they do not like or with people with whom they do not get along, at the end of the day it's a relief to be done with work. A lot of times the stress they experience all day in either holding back their feelings or just making it to the next hour is taken out on the people at home. Here is an opportunity to impact others.

When my husband worked for a boss who was a back-stabber, he would come home irritable, frustrated, and annoyed. It was only after we both attended a workshop by another professional speaker, Dave Yoho, that my husband began to look at his boss as someone who was "just doing the best he could even though it was not very good." And at that point my husband's whole demeanor changed and our marriage was back on track.

Wright

Dave's great, isn't he?

Carver

Yes, do you know him?

Wright

Oh yes.

Carver

This is the father not the son.

Wright

I know the father, yes.

Carver

Okay, well we attended his workshop and it was one of the best things we have done.

Wright

You know, someone told me one day if you're walking down the road and you find a turtle sitting up on a fencepost you can bet he didn't get up there by himself. So who has been a role model for you in your career and in your life?

Carver

There are two people who have been my role models and very influential in my career and in my life. The first person was my grandmother and the second person is my husband.

My grandmother raised me while my mother worked to support us, so she was more of a mother to me. I always admired her because she overcame extreme hardships that gave her strength and courage to continue on. When she was sixteen years old she traveled alone from Poland to the United States to be with her father who was already here. This was during World War I. She was escaping the pogroms but lost her mother and one sister. When she came to New York, all she had was a suitcase and a desire to start a new life in a new world. She had to learn English and make a living. Even though she was not formally educated she learned to survive. She worked and eventually came to own grocery stores in Washington, D.C. Her legacy to me was that I would one day own a business. This was the reason I knew I would be successful as a business owner. Grandma was my hero for twenty-five years until she died in my arms at the age of eighty-two.

My second role model, my husband Carver, impressed me when we first met because he was so intelligent and humorous. My mother and grandmother had always encouraged me to spend time with older people so I could learn from them and Carver fit the bill. He is twelve years my senior and during the past thirty years that we have been married, I have constantly learned new things from him.

In his working life he started out as a physicist, then he moved successfully into management and now he is retired with his own business doing woodcarving. In all his transitions, he exceeded others' expectations and was very good at what he did. It is his influence that has made me strive to be great at what I do. Therefore, I am constantly striving to be better and not settle for mediocre. I learned to play up my strengths so that my weaknesses wouldn't hold me back.

Grandma and Carver have helped mold me to be the person I am today.

Wright

Our marriages are much the same. I'm eleven years older than my wife but we part in the area of intelligence—I think my wife's got me beat by a whole lot.

Carver

I doubt that David—you can't be the owner of a business and not be smart; it's just that your intelligence is in a different area.

Wright

So what hills have you had to climb over? What obstacles have you had to overcome?

Carver

Well, probably the one that stands out in my mind the most is when I was trying to get my business school approved by the government and having to work through that bureaucracy. I needed to have approval by the State Board for Higher Education before I could call my business a school.

The Board assigned me to someone based on the type of school I was starting and his job was to help me get all the needed documentation ready to present to the approving committee. Unfortunately for me, this individual did not appear to be very well versed in what I needed to do to get approval to operate as a school. He would tell me to do one thing and I would do it; then he'd turn around and say it was not what I should have done.

At one point I got very frustrated in dealing with this person and turned to my husband to help me, which is an example of why he is my role model. I didn't trust my ability to keep my cool, so Carver talked with him and was able to get the ball rolling again. Of course, I requested to work with someone else and was assigned another person who understood my frustration with that previous individual. Finally after nine months of working through the system, I did get my full approval and never had problems after that episode. That really was the hurdle that stands out in my mind as the biggest one I have had to face. There have been many other obstacles, but that one was just a very good learning experience for me.

Wright

So what lessons have you learned along the way?

Carver

There are three lessons that have helped me along the way. My first lesson was that fear of failure is a great motivator for me—it has driven me to strive for success. I never feared success but I *did* fear failure and even famous people have had series of failures. An example that comes to mind is Abe Lincoln and his long list of failures before becoming our sixteenth President.

A lot of entrepreneurs have had many failures but kept going. In 1927 Walt Disney tried to get MGM studios to distribute Mickey Mouse but was told the idea would never work because a giant mouse on the screen would terrify women. Jack Canfield and Victor Hansen, the authors of the *Chicken Soup for the Soul* series, went to 140 different publishers and were denied by each one based on the theory that there would not be an audience for this type of writing. Finally a small publishing house thought it was worth the risk and the rest is history. If they had quit early on, we would not have all those great stories. The lesson from that was to never give up.

For me, though, I'll do anything possible to avoid failing. I once tried golfing and decided it was no fun because I could not seem to hit the ball hard enough to go anywhere except in the woods. If I had experienced even a little success, I might have pursued it further and perhaps taken lessons. (I might one day since I know it's such a popular sport requiring a lot of discipline.) It is the fear of failure that drives me to work harder and smarter to make my businesses successful. The thought of not having money to pay my staff really motivates me!

The second lesson I have learned is to find an expert in the skills I did not have. I know I cannot be an expert in everything which is why I have developed the mentality that if it needs to be done and I'm not good at doing it, I'll get someone else to do it for me. It really is a matter of managing my time more effectively. If the task is something I need to learn, then I will take the time to do that. If it is something that I only need once, then my time is better spent on something else. This is how I deal with computer problems, since I am not an expert. If I can't figure out what is wrong in just a few minutes, rather than waste my time I go to the experts who can usually find the problem quickly. It is worth the cost since my time is also worth money.

The third lesson I've learned is to control my anger. If I had said what I really wanted to say about that government bureaucrat when I was trying to get approval for my school, I probably wouldn't have received approval to operate. At that moment I knew the best thing for me was to just walk away and compose myself. More people get in trouble when they say things while they are angry than if they just take a few minutes to compose themselves, rethink the situation, and then come back. Today we call that emotional intelligence or EQ ("Emotional Quotient").

So I think those are the three main lessons I've learned from my experiences.

Wright

I'm interested in your opinion of passion. What part does passion play in someone becoming truly successful?

Carver

For me passion is paramount for success. If I'm not passionate about something, I usually cannot get very interested in doing it. When I am passionate everyone around me knows it because of my voice inflection and my body language. I aspire to inspire and when I see that happening in others it pulls me along more.

Some people don't like to express their emotions and it's hard to know what they are thinking so I usually ask them. I find they are more open then because they see I am truly interested in their response. When talking with some successful people, they seem to have a twinkle in their eye and they get excited about whatever it is they've accomplished. Ask most parents about their children and they're delighted to have the opportunity to start bragging about their child's accomplishments. If they are grandparents, they have an even more intense zeal.

Not all people express their excitement as outwardly as extroverts do but they can still possess it and use it to help them succeed. So I really do think that passion is important in being successful because it gives you that motivation to keep pushing, especially when faced with obstacles.

Wright

Well, this is kind of like a chicken-and-the-egg question: Which do you believe comes first—the passion or the success?

Carver

Some people can be successful without much passion. For example, when someone is born into wealth they may define themselves as successful based on their wealth because they can buy whatever they want; but are they passionate? I don't think so, or at least not to the same degree that someone who worked hard to get where they are is passionate.

For me passion drives me to achieve my goals. When I decide I want to do something or be someone, I strive to do or be the best I can—it is the strong desire that gets me to that point. When I am in the right environment (i.e., surrounded by people or animals), my passionate zeal kicks in.

The best example of this is right before I go on the platform to teach. I could be feeling bad, or down, or depressed but when that first person walks in, my entire demeanor changes and passion takes over. Another person who works with me said she could tell I was in my element one day when I was running an annual job fair for the Army and going around talking with all the employers to make sure they had everything they needed. My passion for what I was doing was evident and the event was a great success.

One of my college professors, Dr. Robert Peters, used to say to me, "Success breeds success," and I believe that to be true. I think that passion and success can occur simultaneously.

Wright

I don't know if I'm just strange or there's something wrong with me but when I meet someone who is supposedly successful and they have no sense of humor, I can never call them a true success. What do you feel about that? Is humor important?

Carver

You bet it is. I started attending an annual humor conference in Saratoga Springs, New York, in 1997 and I have consistently attended each year since. I've come to realize just how important humor is in terms of our health, our career, and our ability to cope with life. Humor can be in many forms—it doesn't have to just be a joke. I use humor in my talks by playing off what the audience says; but you can find humor everywhere if you're open to it. It is in newspaper headlines, on bumper stickers, it can be found on signs in stores, television bloopers, comedy shows, books, Post-it® Notes, watching people or animals, talking with someone who is funny, and on and on.

I go back to Abraham Lincoln and think if he did not have a sense of humor, he would have quit long before he became President. His list of failures or setbacks spans from 1832 when he lost a job and was defeated for state legislature to 1860 when he was finally elected to the U.S. Presidency. Along the way he failed in business, had a nervous breakdown, was defeated for Speaker, defeated for nomination for Congress, defeated for U.S. Senate, and defeated in his bid for Vice-presidency nomination. He finally did get the Vice-presidency, and I believe his sense of humor carried him through.

In an article in *Human Resources* magazine in 1994 a survey of human resources managers said they needed to institute programs that help employees learn to lighten up. A good example of this concept about humor is the Southwest Airlines CEO, Herb Kelleher. His attitude on hiring was revealed when he said, "What we are looking for first and foremost is a sense of humor—we hire attitudes." If you have ever flown on Southwest Airlines, you know what he means. A sense of humor is very important to being successful if not just surviving life—that's successful by itself.

Wright

Right. How did you get into your profession and what credentials are needed?

Carver

Well, I was very fortunate to know that when I started first grade my chosen profession was teaching. The thought of standing in front of a room and imparting my knowledge of a subject just excited me. When I was growing up, instead of playing dolls, I played teacher using my closet door as my chalkboard.

The only time I had second thoughts was when I did my student teaching and had a rude awakening. I discovered I had not been taught how to handle discipline. For a brief moment I wondered if I really wanted to teach. I decided that I did but I would work in private business schools instead of public schools. So I took a possible obstacle and turned it into a stronger commitment for the profession.

A public speaker does not need any specific educational credentials; but having an MBA sure does help with my credibility. One of my customers gives more value to being a practitioner in the field rather than the degrees one holds. There are many people who end up in public speaking simply by what happened to them. For instance, Lisa Beamer, wife of Todd Beamer who was killed in the plane crash in Pennsylvania on 9/11, became an author and speaker almost overnight after that event. Coaches of successful sports teams tend to be requested as motivational speakers with no prior experience or educational preparation. The only real credential you need is something to say that is worth listening to and a great way to say it.

Wright

So why are you so successful?

Carver

Good question. I believe I'm successful because I work at it every day and it's something that I want. I do what I love and love what I do and that is the essence of my success. When I'm working it's more like playing and someone even pays me to do it! I'm driven toward professional success. It is important to me and it is a priority.

Wright

If a movie were made of your life, what type of movie would it be and whom would you choose to star in it?

Carver

Barbra Streisand would be the star and it would be a musical comedy. I chose a comedy because of the value of humor in our lives to which I just alluded. If I'm going to watch a movie, I look for comedies or musicals because they are my favorites. Living with Carver has definitely provided many opportunities to laugh.

My philosophy on viewing problems is to look at them as opportunities, to learn something new, or find some creative way to solve them. When finally discovering electricity Thomas Edison said, "I have not failed 10,000 times. I've just found 10,000 ways it won't work." Barbra is my hero because I sure do wish I had a singing voice like hers.

I also travel a great deal for my business and everyone asks how I handle it. My response is that traveling is an adventure I look forward to. Even waiting for long periods in boring airports can be turned around as an opportunity to explore the environment, watch people, or do some good reading. After the 9/11 disaster traveling did become a little more challenging, but I just go with the flow and don't let it upset me. When I've had problems with luggage not arriving with me, I view it as a chance to buy new clothes!

Wright

I bet Carver loves that!

Carver

Oh yes; but to avoid a possible problem, I try to travel in something I would be willing to wear the next day in front of an audience. So that would be my movie and Barbra would be my hero.

Wright

So your husband is a physicist with a sense of humor?

Carver

Can you believe that!

Wright

That in itself is a story! Well, what a great conversation. I really appreciate your taking all this time with me this morning to talk about this serious subject of success. I believe our readers will really get a lot of information and help from what you said today.

Carver

Great, I hope so, too, because it is something toward which we can all strive.

Wright

Today we've been talking with Darlene T. Carver. She is founder and "Queen Bee" of Merlin & Associates, a training and consulting firm. She inspires people to acquire strong communication and problem-solving skills and, as we have found out here, to acquire these skills with a lot of humor.

Darlene, thank you for being with us today on *Masters of Success*.

About The Author

Darlene T. Carver has been training for over thirty years. She has successfully created two businesses, the first one is a postsecondary business school, which she sold in 1989, and the second is her current training/consulting firm. Her client list includes corporations, colleges/universities, and government. Darlene helps others succeed through her motivational workshops and speeches. She has a BS in Business Education, an MBA, and is a member of the National Speakers Association.

Darlene T. Carver

Merlin & Associates, Inc.

3501 Big Woods Road

Ijamsville, MD 21754

Phone: 301.831.9151

Fax: 301.865.6464

Email: merlin@fred.net

Chapter Thirteen

JANINE DRIVER

David E. Wright (Wright)

Today we're talking with Janine Driver, body language expert, author, and public speaker. Whether you're an employee, a manager, or "the boss," your success depends on how well you connect with other people through verbal and non-verbal communication. No one teaches this skill better than Janine, also known as the "Lyin' Tamer." Her combination of body language and deception detection expertise, rapport building, business coaching, and stand-up comedy inspires, challenges, and energizes individuals from all walks of life. Along with her corporate training and public speaking engagements, Janine is also a regular contributor to *Justice* magazine.

Janine, welcome to *Masters of Success*!

Janine Driver (Driver)

Thank you David, it's nice to be here.

Wright

So, why do people call you the "Lyin' Tamer"?

Driver

Well, I've been dubbed the Lyin' Tamer because I've become pretty adept over the years at recognizing when people are being less than truthful. This skill grew out of my ten years experience of teaching advanced interviewing and detecting deception techniques to law enforcement officials. Not to mention, I've also been trained by the "best in the business," namely deception detection expert psychologists Dr. Paul Ekman from the University of California and Dr. Mark Frank from the State University of New York (SUNY) at Buffalo. And I have been lucky enough to have former Bureau of Alcohol, Tobacco, Firearms, and Explosives (ATF) Special Agent J. J. ("JJ") Newbury, as a mentor. JJ, a.k.a., "The Human Lie Detector," heads the world-renowned Institute of Analytical Interviewing and has coached me in the subtleties of deception detection.

Wright

Well, no matter how beautiful or intelligent you are, I'm glad you are not my wife! How in the world does your husband handle that kind of pressure?

Driver

It's simple. He's in politics, so he is always straightforward and honest (!).

Wright

That's pretty funny! Speaking of your sense of humor, how did you make the transition from being a stand-up comic, who performed with the likes of Chris Rock and Robin Williams, to being a successful public speaker and author?

Driver

You know what, David? I loved doing stand-up comedy. The magic of the stage, the crowd, the laughter—even the occasional heckler—the atmosphere was completely exhilarating. However, the long hours driving from gig to gig, and the dark, dingy bar environment just wasn't a viable, long-term option for me. I knew I wanted to eventually transition to a more stable career (and to marriage and motherhood).

So I bought a book titled, *I Could Do Anything, If Only I Knew What It Was,* by Barbara Sher. I read it from cover to cover and completed the exercises that were in it—every last one! That's when I decided to integrate my stand-up comedy experience, my deception detection skills, as well as my interviewing expertise. The result? A new career as a public speaker!

Once I'd made the decision, a lot of hard work and pavement pounding followed in letting the rest of the world know about my new professional calling. Within a short time, I was fortunate enough to secure several radio and television interview spots, including back-to-back weeks on Fox News. The exposure was outstanding and things took off from there.

Wright

It sounds like you're an extremely busy woman. How do you get so much accomplished?

Driver

Henry David Thoreau once said, "It is not enough to be busy—so are the ants. The question is: what are we busy about?" So often I used to complain that there just was not enough time in the day to accomplish all the things I wanted to achieve. So, I decided to take a good look at how I was spending my hours, minutes, and even seconds!

David, did you know that there are only 8,760 hours in a year?

Wright

No. I don't think I have ever thought about a year in that way!

Driver

Yes, 8,760 hours! And almost 3,000 of those hours are spent sleeping! Therefore, it's much more than just being busy—it's about being focused, goal-oriented, and staying in the game. And if I want to stay in the game, I need to be on the court—not at home in my PJs and flip-flops heckling my television!

Now, here's a task for the readers of this book—what did you spend your 8,760 hours on last year? Was it 500 in traffic, thirty watching *Desperate Housewives*, and forty talking with coworkers about *Desperate Housewives*? (People: stay away from those ladies on Wisteria Lane—they are eating up your precious hours!) Are you using your minutes to move toward what you want in your life? Are you careful to avoid any action that takes you away from your goals and wastes your time?

Wright

Great assignment! Now let's talk about your Lyin' Tamer program, "Read People in Ten Minutes or Less." Do you only offer that course for sales-oriented corporations?

Driver

I actually offer that course to several industries. It benefits sales, real estate, higher education, as well as the medical and legal communities. Occasionally, I also work with recruiters and hiring managers. They have to be excellent in detecting deception—knowing what's behind a resume or when a job candidate is fudging the facts. Figuring out how to read someone in an interview, and being able to quickly tell when there's a hot spot that needs further exploration is also a must!

Recently, I was hired to create a specialized course for a marketing company working with land developers. Since buying a property is a huge investment, a segment of the training discusses Dr. Paul Ekman's seven universal emotions: happiness, sadness, fear, contempt, disgust, anger, and surprise. Learning how to read someone's emotions, especially during a first encounter, is essential to establishing rapport and building trust. A person's face responds to your questions—even if you don't receive an answer in words. (Of course it's important to remember that sometimes your client or date is responding to bad egg salad. It takes practice to know the difference between an emotion and gas.)

I'll be teaching my new marketing clients to focus on how emotions quickly appear or "leak out," so they can address their clients' unspoken concerns. This will ultimately establish immediate rapport and create a positive and trusting first impression with their customers.

Wright

Janine, we've all heard a million times that first impressions last a lifetime. What can our readers do to make sure that they're putting their best foot forward?

Driver

I have five "Lyin' Tamer Quick Tips" for great first impressions I'd like to share with your readers. Can you guess what tops the list? Their walk!

Wright

Their *walk*?

Driver

Yes! It may sound funny, but the first thing I do when I take on a new private client (I'm also a life coach), is watch how she walks. If a client comes in and says, "People think I'm pushy," or, "People think I'm insecure," her walk will quite often give me some important indicators.

I take note of things like people's posture and stride. Their stride and walking pace will reflect their demeanor. Sometimes, if you walk really quickly with feet close together, you'll come across as very confident and determined; however, in a casual setting, you could be perceived as pushy. On the contrary, if you have a wide stance while walking to your boss's office, you may not be taken seriously (think of Bill Murray in *Caddy Shack*). Try walking in both manners down the street and you'll likely feel a different type of attitude.

On the flipside, start observing how other people walk and see if you can make a quick assessment. In the popular book, *Blink,* author Malcom Gladwell calls this "thin-slicing." What does your gut feeling tell you about this person? As the saying goes, "you need to walk before you can run," so I teach my clients the importance of fine-tuning the basics, such as creating a great first impression, before trying to master the more technical communication techniques. (You don't want to be thinking about walking so much that you fall down the stairs like Inspector Clouseau.)

As for the remaining four Lyin' Tamer Quick Tips, I use the acronym "W-A-L-K:"

> **W**et Fish versus Bone Crusher
> **A**nd the Eyes Have it!
> **L**et's Get 'em Talking
> **K**indred Spirits—Mirror Them

Wet Fish versus Bone Crusher

Ah, the handshake. It's unbelievable David, how many people are simply not good at shaking hands. Believe it or not, but the handshake tells a story about each of us. Do you shake hands softly? Do you come from the top and give the "bone crusher handshake"? It may seem overly simplistic, but it really is easy to get off on the wrong foot with a new acquaintance with a bad handshake. A handshake can be soft, firm, brief, long, or even painful. The way you shake hands provides clues to your personality. Aggressive people have firm handshakes. People with low self-esteem often have limp handshakes, also known as the "wet fish." Politicians typically shake your hand with their other hand covering the shake or holding your elbow. Domineering men often squeeze women's hands during a greeting.

What should you do?

For starters, stay away from using the "bone crusher" and avoid the "wet fish." The trick to a great handshake is to find a happy medium between the two—somewhere between Hulk Hogan and Woody Allen. Creating the right impression with your handshake is a three-step process:

1. Make sure your hands are clean and adequately manicured.
2. Your hands should also be warm and free of perspiration.
3. Execute your handshake professionally and politely, with a firm grip and warm smile.

And the Eyes Have it!

When you meet someone for the first time, look him or her right in the eyes. It's well known that when we look at someone we find attractive, our pupils dilate. It's a phenomenon the other person instinctively picks up on, a subconscious reaction, if you will. What people should do when they meet someone during a business function or in a personal setting is look them in the eyes, then say to yourself in your mind, "Wow, so great to meet you!" What will happen is that you'll involuntarily smile and the other person will pick up on your positive mood.

Let's Get 'em Talking

Focus on the other person. If you're doing all the talking, you're actually not the person in control. What you want to do is get the other person engaged. Simply focus the conversation on them by asking open-ended questions, such as "How" questions: "How do you like living in Alexandria?" "How is your current home owner's insurance company working for you?" "How would you prefer to communicate with your customers?" Quite frankly, when you focus the conversation on the other person, it takes the pressure off you. And let's face it—people love to talk about themselves!

Kindred Spirits—Mirror Them

People like people who are like themselves. By "mirroring" the person with whom you're communicating, you'll quickly become a kindred spirit. Adjust your posture, voice, and hand gestures to those of your new acquaintance. By mirroring his body rhythms and speaking at his preferred pace or volume, you'll help establish rapport. For instance, I'm really a high-pitched, excited type of a speaker, but if I'm speaking with someone who is more soft-spoken, I'll mirror her voice, tone, and mannerisms. The person will subconsciously think, "There is something about Janine that I can relate to—she *gets* me!" Remember to make it look natural. Don't make them think they've stumbled into that famous mirror scene in the Marx brothers' movie, *Duck Soup!*

Now, let's summarize: My five Lyin' Tamer Quick Tips to help people put their best foot forward are: 1) Watch Your WALK, 2) Wet Fish versus Bone Crusher, 3) And the Eyes Have it! 4) Let's Get 'em Talking, and 5) Kindred Spirits—Mirror Them. You know, David, you can only make a first impression once, so by getting the basics right, you'll leave your audience wanting more.

Wright

Janine, you have a proven track record of enhancing the way businesses communicate within their organization and with their customers. Will you share with our readers some of your Lyin' Tamer "Reach the ROOF of Success" secrets?

Driver

Ah, yes—the ever-popular "Reach the ROOF of Success," otherwise known as the **"R-O-O-F!"**

> **R**apport
> **O**bserve & Listen
> **O**utcome & Intention
> **F**lexibility

Rapport

Building rapport is a true fundamental; without it you have no open lines of communication. As I said earlier, people like people who are like themselves. So, when establishing rapport with a person, try to find something the two of you have in common. And don't forget to mirror them, ask open-ended questions, and say the person's name.

Here are two more proven Lyin' Tamer tips you can use to establish rapport:

1. **Smile and pay the other person a compliment.** For instance, pick out something on her office wall or compliment his tie or his nicely polished shoes. Practice your technique by complimenting strangers just for fun, like people in the grocery store, or the lady in front of you in the bank.
2. **Be interested and attentive.** Put your cell phone on vibrate and ignore other distractions. Maintain eye contact to show that you are really interested.

Observe & Listen

The famous British detective, Sherlock Holmes said, "You see, but you do not observe." Do you know what your boss is telling you in the boardroom when she has her hand over her mouth? Does your significant other's body gestures match his verbal responses? Are you aware of the message your client is telling you when he rubs the back of his neck, or when she rubs her palms together when you are ready to negotiate?

Psychologists claim that the impact you make on others depends on what you say (seven percent), how you say it (thirty-eight percent), and by your body language (fifty-five percent). This means that ninety-three percent of emotion is communicated without actual words. According to the above, more than half of what we communicate with others is non-verbal—body language. Have you been observing people's body language? Do you notice when someone deviates from his or her norm (normal behavior)? Is there a hot spot you've noticed? When someone shifts from normal behavior patterns to something else, explore what's going on there by both observing and listening. Also, look for groups of signals that all have the same meaning. Does the body language match what the person is saying? It should also match the context of the situation. So look for body language in clusters of signals with common meanings.

For instance, ABC's Primetime Live ran an interesting story regarding the Kobe Bryant rape case, where he was charged with sexual assault (the charges were later dropped). The Primetime interview was of a college student, who knew the accuser intimately. He was also working at the hotel as a bellman, the night of the alleged rape. During the interview the interviewee was confident, articulate, and calm. However, when asked if he had sexual relations with Bryant's accuser, he made a dramatic shift in his chair, turned his body (away from the interviewer), and reached on the ground for a glass of water. This is what I would call a "Hot Spot." He deviated from his normal behavior. This would be an area to explore further with the interviewee.

David, the point is that being aware of body language cues, signals, and hot spots that are being sent to you by others is a crucial skill if you want to master your communication skills and reach the "ROOF of Success." After all, if you are unaware of what others are telling you with their body language, you could be missing out on what is really going on, so be sure to carefully observe and listen.

Outcome & Intention

According to the author of *The Power of Intentions*, Dr. Wayne Dyer, "We become what we think about all day long. The question is, 'What do you think about?'" Research has shown that expected outcomes and intentions correlate with actual behavior and results.

David, allow me to share a personal experience with you. Five years ago, I was living with my sister, Caileen. After trudging home late from work one night, I began feeling especially lonely and sorry for myself. As it so happened, I'd also fallen into the nasty habit of blaming everyone but myself for the choices in my life. That particular night, I took it out on Caileen. Within an hour of arriving home, my sister looked at me and said, "Why are you being so bitchy tonight?"

After digesting the shock of hearing my own sister tell me I was bitchy, I replied, "It's just that I am heavy, my clothes don't fit, I'm lonely, and I want to cry! Caileen I am really, really fat!"

She looked at me very seriously with a twinkle of near-compassion in her eyes and said, "Um, yeah, you were fat last week...but at least you weren't a bitch!"

The room fell silent. Then came the outburst of hysterical laughter from both of us and my Zen moment of realization that Caileen was completely right. That same day I chose to stop complaining and I created the possibility of success, opportunity, and abundance. Yes, I took control over my life and the direction it was heading. Soon afterward I lost sixty pounds, got a new job, and smiled more. Six months later, I met the love of my life, Leif Larson, on match.com.

What is your expected or desired outcome of this job interview? What is the outcome of this business negotiation? What do you hope to gain from reading this book, *Masters of Success*? What is it that *you* want?

Flexibility

You need to be flexible in your communication style because every person you encounter is different and may process information differently. One way to work on this is by becoming more aware of how to read people, how to pick up on different body language and emotional cues, and determine others' preferences for processing information (through pictures, sounds, or feelings.) A fun way to practice this is to take a friend to the mall or to a crowded restaurant or bar and try to read people's body language from across the room.

Again, to reach the "ROOF of Success" just remember R-O-O-F: Rapport, Observe & Listen, Outcome & Intention, and Flexibility.

Wright

So Janine, will you give us your top three suggestions on how companies or individuals can improve their non-verbal communication?

Driver

Top three? Absolutely!

One: If you can't agree with someone in a conversation, you need to control your body language so that a negative gesture will not reveal itself. Instead, grab a pen and make a note. It's an amazingly powerful tool if you can just divert your eye contact long enough to write something down and prevent that negative micro-expression from leaking out.

Two: When you are talking with someone and you are receptive for others to join your conversation, be sure that you and your conversational mate both open your body posturing/stance at least thirty degrees. I call this the "door hinge theory." Open the door at least thirty degrees, and let the world know you are open for business. (NOTE: If you do *not* want others to interrupt, be sure to have your belly button face the belly button of your partner. This "closed door" will tell others, you are in a private conversation.)

Three: Be conscious of gestures and substitute better gestures for negative ones.

To be a successful communicator, you must be aware of the signals you are sending others. For instance, even though you may be interested in the person speaking with you, if you cross your arms because it is comfortable for you to sit that way, the other person may think you are closed, bored, or disinterested. Therefore it is vital that you pay close attention to what signals you are sending others. Your ability to recognize what your body language may be saying to others can mean the difference between making a great impression or a very bad one.

Controlling your body language will help you to establish rapport and build trust with your clients, supervisors, employees, family members, and date mates—basically, everyone.

Commonly Recognized Negative Body Language Gestures:

- Poor eye contact (less than sixty percent)
- Rubbing thumb over thumb
- Biting fingernails
- Hands in pockets
- Hand covering mouth while speaking
- Wringing hands
- Arms and ankles crossed
- Playing with hair
- Clearing throat
- Whistling
- Swaying
- Fidgeting in chair
- Jingling money in pockets

Commonly Recognized Positive Body Language Gestures:

- Smile
- Tilted head
- Head nods
- Leaning forward
- Open hands, palms facing out
- Sitting on edge of chair
- Unbuttoned coat

Wright

I remember that famous take of President Bush—the first President Bush—when he looked at his watch while debating Clinton. Big mistake!

Driver

Right. And did you know the reason he looked at his watch, David? It's because he couldn't see a clock nearby and was thinking that Clinton was getting more than his allotted time! Now, most viewers watching the televised broadcast saw something entirely different— some saw an arrogant man too good for the debate, while others thought Bush looked like he was in a rush to get out of there. Sometimes, even an event as significant as an election can be lost, in part, by unfavorable body language cues.

Wright

You mentioned earlier that you've studied with some of the world's expert authorities on verbal and non-verbal behavior attributed to deceptive people. Will you give our readers a couple of your "Lyin' Tamer" quick tips on how deceptive people reveal themselves?

Driver

Sure, but before I divulge any secrets I must share with you that it's incredibly difficult to know if someone is lying unless you have prior exposure to his or her normal behavior, also called a baseline. You must know how they normally act so you can spot when there is a deviation in their normal behavior (tone of voice, hand gestures, facial expressions, eye contact, body rhythms, etc.). With that said, here are three tells that are scientifically proven through Dr. Paul Ekman's research:

One: A shoulder shrug paired with a definitive statement. An example of a definitive statement is if I say, "Lunch breaks should be an hour long." Here, I'm putting forth a position in no uncertain terms. As I'm saying this, if I do a quick little shoulder shrug, the shrug tells an observer, "Um, I don't know." Now if my answer was, "I don't know if lunch breaks should be longer than thirty minutes," then the shrug would make more sense. The bottom line? If someone is making a definitive statement and shrugging at the same time, it's an indicator they're being less than truthful. You'd want to explore that hot spot a little more.

Two: Shaking one's head in the wrong direction. Perhaps the most infamous example of this was Clinton's "I did not have sexual relations with that woman" statement, which he paired with an affirmative (up-and-down) slight head nod and a pointed index finger also going up-and-down. Shaking your head in the opposite direction from what you're saying indicates to others that you're being untruthful. So, if you're trying to read someone, when in doubt, trust their body language cues over their actual words. As the great American artist Robert Henri once said, "If you want to know about people, watch their gestures. The tongue is a greater liar than the body."

Three: The use of "stalling techniques." When people repeat your question, stutter, stammer, clear their throats, etc., they are stalling. It doesn't necessarily mean they're lying, but it may be a hot spot worthy of exploration. An example is if I ask, "Where were you last night David?" and you respond, "Where was I last night?" Another example is televised interviews when politicians are asked, "Were you at lunch with x, y, or z?" and they clear their throat and sip a glass of water. What's happening when someone is using a stalling technique is that they're deciding: "Am I going to lie?" Or, if they are going to lie, "What will I say?"

So, in summary, my top three items on the "indicators of untruthfulness" list are: (1) shoulder shrug that goes along with a definitive statement, 2) shaking the head in the opposite direction to a spoken statement, and 3) use of stalling techniques.

Wright

Janine, what exactly is the *truth* anyway?

Driver

Another great question! Have you ever heard of the story about the blind men measuring the elephant?

Wright

No, but you have peeked my curiosity.

Driver

To one blind man touching the elephant's side, the creature seemed "very much like a wall." The other, grasping the trunk, described the elephant as decidedly "snake-like." So which is the *truth*? Is the elephant solid, flat, and stationary like a wall or is it thin, flexible, and extremely mobile like a snake? My point being, the truth is what we believe to be true. Two people can witness a car accident and describe what happened in two completely different ways, one story even contradicting the other story. Which person would you call the *liar*? Again, the truth is what *we* believe to be true.

Wright

I can only imagine how many people have been called a liar when in fact they truly believed that what they were saying was the truth.

Driver

David, it's like Dr. Wayne Dyer says, "Change the way you look at things, and the things you look at change!"

Wright

Janine, not only are you a body language and deception detection expert, but you also are a Certified Life Coach. As a life coach, how do you go about solving people's problems?

Driver

"*I*" don't solve people's "problems." See David, the coaching process assumes that my clients are resourceful and capable of providing their own solutions. I don't consider them broken like an old Chevy up on cinderblocks. To the contrary, the coaching process actually enables my clients to discover their strengths and raises their awareness of how they function as a person. I believe *they* are their own experts, with all of the answers to their own questions. Throughout my coaching engagements, my clients decide on areas for development and define their own goals and objectives. Then, I work with them to access behavioral models, capture key action steps, check progress, and highlight key insights.

My business and life coaching provides unique opportunities for individuals and companies searching for growth, change, and success. No two coaching sessions are the same. Having said that, there are some general similarities, which I'll share with your readers:

One: *Outcome*. What do you want and how will you know when you've achieved it? What's your evidence of success?

Two: *Current situation*. Define what is happening right now. What is the operating strategy that maintains limiting behavior and what is the motivation that keeps things repeating (and therefore the same)?

Three: *Long-term effects*. Change inevitably creates impact, and being aware of this in advance is vital to the coaching process. Long-term effects not only impact you, but also others in your life.

So outcome, current situation, and long-term effects—those constitute the basics in my initial sessions, and are a recurring theme in the sessions that follow. Surprisingly, there are times when just one coaching session is enough to help a person answer these questions, resulting in a commitment to behavioral change and a new direction in life.

Wright

What are some of the coaching tools you provide individuals and business professionals with, so that they may build a successful career and fulfilling personal life?

Driver

I'll give you two of my favorite exercises:

One: *Create a five-minute habit.* What can you do for five minutes a day that can change who you are? Here's an example: Each weekday morning, my parents would rush off to work in separate cars each drinking their morning hot beverage—my mom with her tea and my dad with his coffee. Their five-minute habit? Before hopping into their cars, they now sit down outside or in their sunroom and enjoy looking at their beautiful garden. Instead of leaping right into their workday, they share a little time together. Then, they begin their day renewed and refreshed before facing whatever lies ahead.

Another example: A client of mine used to turn on the news as soon as she walked in the front door of her house after a long day of work. This created more stress in her life. So she created a five-minute habit of coming home and listening to her favorite music CD for five minutes before doing anything else. She credits this little five-minute change to lowering her high blood pressure and decreasing her stress. So what simple five-minute habit can *you* create that can change *your* life?

Two: *Get an "accountability buddy."* Get a friend or coworker who is also trying to create some change in his or her life. In every organization—corporations, nonprofit, schools, churches, and even families—there is blame, complaining, and procrastination. Having a partner means you can hold one another accountable and actually *do* the things you say you are going to do!

Wright

Those are some great ideas! Would you tell our readers, before we wrap up, about what drives you to be a master of success?

Driver

I would love to! First, I'll tell you about a remarkable man—an amazing professor I met during my studies at North Adams State College. His name is Dr. Harris Elder. One time, after I made a somewhat over-the-top (but pretty darn funny!) farewell tribute to a departing alumni employee, Harris said to me, "Janine Driver, you can do anything. You're going to be a millionaire some day." Even though I was only twenty-two years old at the time, I really hung on to those words; they have pushed me to believe that anything is possible.

It was then that I quickly learned to become what I like to call "unreasonable." See, most people are too reasonable and that holds them back from being extraordinary. We all have reasons why we can't be millionaires, reasons why we can't lose weight, reasons why our companies will never be on the Fortune 500 list—that's what I call being "reasonable." When I set a lofty goal and negative reasons why it's unattainable quietly tiptoe in, I remind myself that I am being "reasonable." Then, I follow through with (and usually obtain!) my unreasonable goal anyway.

Here's an example that literally changed my life's course: I knew early on that I wanted to become more involved in the deception detection field and ultimately work with J. J. Newberry. So, one day, I called him up and said, "Hi, my name is Janine Driver and I am a body language expert. I would like to be the next J. J. Newberry." At first he seemed caught off guard, but weeks later, we set up a meeting in Washington, D.C., and have been great friends ever since. He's an incredible mentor.

See, my secret is to filter out all those negative thoughts and the cautionary advice of those who dwell on why it can't be done. Instead, I rely on my own inner voice and belief system to carry me past any obstacles. I truly believe there's nothing I can't do. That's my message from Dr. Harris Elder.

Next, what is my energy secret? Not only do I believe in myself and my unstoppable spirit, but I am also lucky enough to have purpose and passion behind my actions. I love helping ordinary people attain extraordinary results. This generates an unbelievable amount of energy for me. I have a life I love and every day I look forward to exploring what's ahead of me and sharing it with others.

Do *you* have a life that *you* love?

In a related story, my mom, Lorraine, a registered nurse and life coach, was chatting with a nursing co-worker one day about coaching. She explained to the woman how coaches can help people get a clearer sense of what they want in their lives by asking powerful questions. The nurse didn't say much in response, and likely thought to herself, "I love my life and don't need to over-think it." It wasn't until three weeks later that my mother realized the true impact of their conversation.

At seven in the morning, my mom arrived on the second floor of Mount Auburn Hospital only to hear the sad news that her coworker had quit. But to my mom's surprise, there was a handwritten card waiting for her, explaining the reasons behind the nurse's choice and thanking her. After speaking with my mom about coaching, the nurse told herself that she already had a life she loved. But later that night and in the days to follow, she started to take a closer look at the *quality* of her life. Since she worked the rigorous 11 P.M. until 7 A.M. shift, she had no time or energy to see her boyfriend and rarely saw her friends anymore. When the weekends arrived she was too exhausted to stay active, so she often just caught up on lost hours of sleep. Realizing this actually wasn't the life she wanted, the nurse immediately began applying for jobs at other hospitals where she could work the morning shift *and* have the fulfilling personal life she so craved. The letter ended with words of thanks to my mother for being the catalyst to this life-altering change.

Now let me ask you again, do *you* have a life *you* love?

Last but not least, I'll tell you about a somewhat sappy but motivational song titled, "I Get Knocked Down," by the British group ChumbaWumba. The chorus goes: "I get knocked down, but I get up again, nothing's gonna hold me down."

While in New York City in the mid-nineties with comedian friends Terry Moore and Poppi Kramer, the three of us would drive from comedy club to comedy club, looking for stage time. When that song came on the radio, I'd just belt it out and sing LOUD, because, you know what? No one wins *all* the time and setbacks are inevitable. Nothing's going to hold me down and I truly believe that! When I get knocked down, I get up again—and I'm that much stronger for it.

Wright

A great man told me one time, back in the sixties, that the definition of a champion is the person who gets up one more time than he falls down.

Driver

Right. And along the same lines, my Nana used to say, "If you don't give up, you simply cannot fail."

Wright

What a great conversation, Janine! It's been awesome getting a quick peak into your success.

Driver

Thank you David. It's been a lot of fun! Janine Driver, Lyin' Tamer, over-and-out!

About The Author

Janine Driver, Lyin' Tamer, has combined her insightful body language and deception detection analysis and comedic talent to become one of the most sought after public speakers in the business world. Janine's expertise and fascinating work/life stories have been highlighted on Fox News Live, CBS Sunday Morning Show, Hard Copy, E!, and in *Justice* magazine. Janine is married to political media consultant Leif Larson. They live in Alexandria, Virginia, with their newborn son, Angus Joseph.

Janine Driver, Lyin' Tamer

4603 Eaton Place, Suite 143

Alexandria, VA 22310

202-271-0922

Janine@Lyintamer.com

www.lyintamer.com

Chapter Fourteen

GLEN MILLER

THE INTERVIEW

David E. Wright (Wright)

Today we're talking with Glen Miller. Glen is a performance improvement consultant providing expertise in culture and process change. As a consultant, Glen supports organizational change through improved innovation, creativity, and leadership.

As a speaker, Glen draws on his experience as an Army ranger, a parent, department manager, and consultant to tell humorous and powerful stories that dramatically illustrate principles of effective leadership, creativity, and personal fulfillment. His speech, *Playing for Money,* includes paradoxical and irreverent stories regarding the difficulties of unleashing the creative talents of managers and employees. In *Creating a Living,* Glen elaborates on the notion that every individual has a special calling.

Glen, welcome to *Masters of Success*!

Glen Miller (Miller)

Thank you for having me here!

Wright

What is your current business?

Miller

My current business is organizational change, with some speaking engagements. The current change project that I'm on is part of an overall strategy for a family of companies in the ground beef business—that's right, they make hamburger. They're profitable and growing, in no small part because upper management has a vision and mission and they're continually developing their leadership team.

The strategic work of developing their vision and mission is very interesting and fulfilling to me—I worked with them on that. The company executives really worked through what their primary purpose was and how they would sustain growth for the betterment of the company and their customers.

Then they further demonstrated their commitment by contracting me to design and teach a three-day leadership academy that includes everyone in management from their general managers on through to their team leaders. The leadership academy is designed to meet one immediate need—for managers and supervisors to become ready to move up or into other leadership positions.

The second goal for the academy is to ensure that all managers and supervisors have time to interpret and modify the company vision and mission, so they get some buy-in and are able to play around with the ideas. The second goal has been implemented and every leadership academy has a project. Each group designs a presentation and interprets the vision and mission. It's been really helpful in ensuring that the entire management team has had an opportunity to challenge, discuss, and interpret the vision for the company.

This leadership team has also addressed the biggest threat to their business success, which is food safety. Not only do they have a great food safety program, but they also make sure their leaders and employees know how important the food safety program is to the business and the well-being of their customers.

Wright

Before we dive into the specifics of some of your projects, interests, and views, will you give our readers a brief description of how you came to be a speaker and change agent?

Miller

Sure. My career path has been more bends than straight lines. I believe I started toward being a change agent after I had experienced war and combat as a twenty-two-year-old. I was a sergeant in an

Army Ranger company. I was the leader on the ground. At the time our patrols were usually made up of six men; we were called L-R-R-Ps, which stands for Long Range Reconnaissance Patrols. War is a life-changing experience; it certainly changed me.

Before my combat experience I was not committed or dedicated to much. I was interested in sports and making money, but after my year in combat I wanted to make a difference and I felt strongly that things could be a lot better. Once back in the world (Vietnam Era vets, by the way, refer to the good old USA as "the world") I found it very difficult to gain employment.

That difficulty led to many different jobs and finally I became a teacher of industrial arts. I loved it. I had to learn so much to teach industrial arts. The young people loved to learn practical things like how a building was constructed or how a toy was manufactured.

I then had the opportunity to teach at Temple University's Industrial Technology Program. The students there were usually older than your typical college student. Many had worked as craftsman or technicians in industry and were taking courses to teach in the public schools, particularly in Philadelphia.

Temple's program was very progressive. The basic idea was that the teachers in industrial arts should use their shops to give young people the opportunity to learn about the world of work. Students were to learn about jobs and the basics of manufacturing, communication, and power technology. This meant fewer projects but more creativity in design and problem-solving. It was hands on career and technology education and the philosophy was different than the prevailing curriculum in the schools. The mainstay of shop in 1975 was practicing a craft such as woodworking, which had little to do with manufacturing, construction, and other technology in the United States at the time. Temple's progressive curriculum gave me great opportunity to be creative and to foster creativity in the college students.

We had one project that we called a "Rube Goldberg." Basically the students had to design a device that incorporated all the simple machines and actually did some work. The University students were very energetic about this problem. They would incorporate elaborate chutes, inclined planes, pulley systems, and levers, just to open a beer can. During a project like that they learned a lot about mechanical and electrical systems and they were creative in their design.

In the long run, however, the traditions of the public schools were difficult to break. Science teachers took the lead in teaching technology and science through a curriculum that explored careers as well as creative problem-solving and eventually the industrial technology program was shut down—I was out of a job. I had a choice to make: stay in education or move out into industry.

I thought I had to get out in the world of business to try to make a difference. The incident at Three Mile Island helped me get my next job. After the accident, nuclear utilities wanted people with knowledge of technology and education; I fit that description. I jumped to nuclear power and in 1987 I got my first chance at big-time change.

Peachbottom Atomic Power Station was shut down as a result of inadequate leadership and arrogance. It was a huge industrial event. No power plant had ever been shut down because of "people's attitudes." Leadership in charge of the plant literally had no idea how to adjust attitudes or change behavior. The utility was losing a million dollars a day during the shutdown. It was a huge problem for the utility but an opportunity for me. I learned a lot about organizational change while I was assigned to the re-start team; I just kept going from there.

My speaking engagements, for example, are an extension of my organizational change business. Sometimes I do a speech for a company I'm already working with, other times a speech may lead to an organizational change project. My favorite topics for speeches are leadership, creativity, and personal fulfillment. These are topics that are important aspects of every change project in which I have worked.

Wright

I read that you have several degrees in different disciplines. Has this helped you in your organizational change projects?

Miller

I have degrees in business, technology, and education, all of which help me have perspective. I basically love to learn and that is why I pursued degrees in different disciplines. My formal education, however, was just a start. I'm still learning and I read every day. One of my favorite quotes is: "We are all ignorant, just about different things."—Will Rogers (1879-1935).

I do not take degrees seriously, however, I do always strive to learn. In business school I studied labor relations and management. So much has changed since I received that degree that I do not think it has really helped me very much. My degree in industrial technology has helped me understand manufacturing and industrial processes.

Now, when I'm in a manufacturing plant, I have a reasonable understanding of how the equipment and processes work. This technical knowledge helps me communicate with the supervisors and workers in particular.

The degree I received in education was mostly about the psychology of learning. I'm interested in how people learn and grow, which has been a big help in realizing how changing an organization of 500 or more people can be so difficult.

My favorite part of learning and thinking is the creative process. While I was at Temple University I did research regarding inventions and how inventors think differently from others. My research on creative thinking has helped me during my organizational change projects—creativity, innovation, and change go hand-in-hand.

Wright

What do you consider success at work?

Miller

Primarily I think work success is working every day on projects that are congruent with your values. It is important to have meaningful work. Meaningful work requires that you know what you value. I, for example, value learning. I am most successful when people become more creative and receptive to change and change themselves because of some part of what my company has initiated and the part I have played in that change.

Another part of success for me is having influence on how programs or change initiatives are designed. I like having input. I also like getting feedback—changing parts of programs and increasing a program's effectiveness.

Wright

When have you felt the most successful?

Miller

When people attending workshops or a leadership academy comment that they have gained food for thought or when someone says that a leadership academy has changed his or her life. The most memorable comment after a workshop was, "If I had to learn to breathe, I would select Glen to teach me."

During organizational change I often lead team-building. When the organization really starts to hum as a team that feels successful. I also feel successful because this is my tenth year of running my own business.

Wright

What part of your business do you enjoy the most?

Miller

I like both parts, namely organizational change and speaking engagements. I have learned so much about how organizations and people change and I factor most of that experience into my speeches. Both parts of the business go together—one isn't complete without the other.

For pure enjoyment I like doing speeches along with immediate dialogue or discussion after each speech. I also really enjoy working directly in a manufacturing environment. I watch, participate, coach, and generally become a catalyst for changing processes. I really enjoy that shop floor part of organizational change.

Not too long ago I helped invent a simple device that saved time setting up some grinding equipment. I was real excited about the device and working with a team to get it in place. The device is a practical, time-saving process improvement. As I was just explaining, I do a lot of process improvement in my business. Strategy needs leadership and continued follow-up in the work area. Most of what is done inside the plant work area is called "lean manufacturing" or "process improvement." The basics of lean manufacturing specify that you have your tools and parts at hand. That sounds easy but those basics need leadership and follow-up to sustain in a manufacturing setting.

Wright

You have two primary speeches: "Creating a Living" and "Playing for Money." Would you tell our readers how you picked those titles and what they are all about?

Miller

Interesting titles. "Creating a Living" started out as "Blazing a Path." I then thought it was way too competitive and aggressive a title. I had images of the bumper sticker: "He with the most toys wins" being handed out after my talk. I then tried, "Finding Your Path," a more low octane approach to "blazing." That did not fit the contemplative theme of what I wanted to communicate. Then I tried

"Creating a Living." That title fit because I was most interested in encouraging people to consider their special gifts. Considering your special gifts and discovering your calling requires contemplation, reflection, and courage to pursue unique career paths.

"Creating a Living" elaborates on the notion that every individual has a special calling. The speech is important for me because I think we forfeit our creativity way too quickly in this land of liberty. Americans have many more options than most other nations. We tend to become possessed by our possessions. We become successful, then we get a raise, and then we buy a bigger house. Eventually it's very hard to leave the job. Perhaps the biggest restraint on creating a living that is truly our signature life is a decent job.

The other title: "Playing for Money" is subtitled: "Creativity in the Workplace." "Playing for Money" refers to the nature of creative endeavor as fun or at least an intrinsically stimulating activity. I basically poke fun at the corporate world's dilemma of coveting creativity while demonstrating apprehension every time a creative approach is offered. I love the paradox of creativity in the workplace.

I even do a skit imitating Albert Einstein in the twenty-first century corporation. Einstein wants to wheel his blackboard into the boardroom to explain $E=MC^2$. His boss wants Albert to go back into his cube and develop a PowerPoint presentation. I'll tell you, the skit's a hoot.

Other than advertising, architecture, and the arts, creativity is often met with apprehension. I've worked primarily with engineers and technical people. They appreciate creativity once it is driven through to effective application. Initially, however, unique and creative ideas, people, or solutions are considered out there or unusual. This view, of course, is the great paradox.

Wright

If you were mentoring a young group of men and women and one of their central goals was to become successful, what advice would you give them?

Miller

Work hard, but take some breaks to examine the meaning that work and your career are bringing into your life. What kinds of conversations do you have every day? Are the relationships bred from work making you explore new and fulfilling ways to live? Are you learning every day or has the work become routine? We spend approximately fifty percent of our waking hours at work; I think we should gain some joy from that time. I think all people need to be in the process of becoming successful. In other words, make sure you're enjoying the journey. This is particularly true for young people. Of course, I'm not at all thinking of bigger and shinier possessions. I tell young people that we are becoming more and more successful when we can feel joy from work well done.

Wright

What new projects are you working on?

Miller

My newest project is career counseling. My speech, "Creating a Living," has drawn some interest in career counseling. So far it has not been profitable, but it feels worthwhile when I can help a young person align their special talents with their interests and the marketplace. I also enjoy helping friends and acquaintances change careers. I have revised "Creating a Living" to a speech subtitled: "Take This Midlife Crisis and Love It." In that version of "Creating a Living" I tell more stories about career shifts after someone has matured doing one type of work. I have interviewed people who have changed from being an office administrator to becoming a naturopath. Another was a lawyer and is now teaching social studies.

When people make changes like this it takes courage and some real soul-searching. I've found that people feel much more alive and successful when they make these kinds of changes. The naturopath, for example, has struggled with financial difficulties but she is in her fifth year and she is making it. Most importantly, she is passionate and joyful about her work as a natural healer.

Perhaps another project will grow out of my interest in mid-life career changes. Perhaps a book of interviews similar to Studs Terkel's classic, *Working...* is on the horizon. I think this interview has clarified that project for me. I want to write a book of interviews featuring people who have uniquely transformed or changed their careers. The book would be titled: *Loving that Mid-life Crisis.* I hope there are stockbrokers out there who have become arborists and engineers who have become dog breeders willing to be interviewed.

Wright

Is there continued success for your future?

Miller

I'm hopeful. I'm taking risks and some are bound to be fruitful. I am succeeding in helping manufacturing companies change. I am writing and speaking on topics that are timeless—creativity and finding your calling. The speeches are becoming more sought after. Most importantly, I am doing work that is meaningful to me and that is helping others. I believe that will be the enduring quality of success.

Wright

Well, what an interesting conversation. I really appreciate your taking all this time with me Glen, to share some of your success for our *Masters of Success* book. Thank you so much for your time.

Miller

Thank you!

Wright

Today we've been talking with Glen Miller. He is a performance improvement consultant providing expertise in process change. As a consultant he supports organizational change through improved innovation, creativity, and leadership and I think after this conversation today, I have determined that he knows what he's talking about. Thanks Glen!

Miller

Thank you David!

About The Author

Glen Miller is an organizational development consultant providing expertise in process change and performance improvement for over twenty-five years. Glen has designed and conducted benchmarking, process improvement, and leadership development in various work environments to enhance the skills and attitudes needed for change, teamwork, and productivity. Recently, Glen has converted his interests in organizational change into inspirational speeches that promote more creativity at work and our daily lives.

Glen Miller

Performance Essentials, Inc.

137 East Woods Drive

Harleysville, PA 19438

Phone: 1.800.513.0601

Email: glenmiller@performanceessentials.com

www.performanceessentials.com

Chapter Fifteen

CHARLOTTE PALMER LANDRAM

David Wright (Wright)

Today we're talking with Charlotte Palmer Landram. Charlotte creates and leads customized training and development programs for companies across the United States and Canada as well as in Australia and the United Kingdom. Her highly effective approach is to combine group education with a series of follow-up coaching sessions with the individual participants. *"The results achieved are four times greater when excellent training is combined with professional coaching,"* says Charlotte.

Charlotte, welcome to *Masters of Success.*

Charlotte Palmer Landram (Landram)

Thank you David.

Wright

What is your definition of coaching?

Landram

Coaching is an intense one-on-one relationship solely focused on helping the client reach his or her maximum level of achievement.

The maximum level of achievement or mastery can only be reached when one allows time to reflect on what he or she is doing and assess if there are areas that need improvement. In my practice, the coaching process provides the client time to momentarily step "out" of the rigors of daily business and work "on" it.

Wright

So why do you feel that coaching is a key component of success?

Landram

To succeed and ultimately master a sport, a hobby, or a profession, an individual must achieve a very high level of competence in a very few key areas. Coaching helps clients identify and define the specific key areas, assess their ability in each area, and then develop a plan to increase their effectiveness. For example, I coach a gentleman who was recently promoted to a sales management position. For many years he was a highly successful salesperson and directly responsible for identifying key prospects and converting them to clients. When we began working together he was having great difficultly in leading his sales organization. He was trying to apply sales skills instead of management skills. Together we identified recruiting, training, and retaining key sales talent as his three key areas of priority or critical competency. In each coaching session we focus on his progress. We designed a plan to improve his skills in each of these three essential areas.

Wright

What do you feel are the characteristics of a great coach?

Landram

David, I can answer that very specifically. There are five core characteristics of a great coach:

1. **Disciplined and effective listening** – Coaching is about great listening, not great speaking. The first coach I hired and then quickly fired was a poor listener. Poor listening communicates to the client that you don't care. If the client perceives that the coach is not listening they will immediately stop communicating fully. Once this occurs an effective coaching relationship is not possible.

2. **Understanding of the client's profession** – A coach who has actual experience in the client's required skill area or profession is ideal. For example, if one wanted to learn to play golf, who would be a better choice of a coach—a retired professional golfer or a retired professional hockey player? They are both successful athletes and they both play a sport; but the retired golfer has a greater understanding of the client's game.

3. **Prompt and prepared consulting** – A great coach is always on time, takes detailed notes during the session, and reviews the notes prior to each appointment.

4. **Respecting the client fully** – The great humanitarian psychologist, Dr. Carl Rogers, believed in giving his clients unconditional positive regard. The coach must respect clients' needs fully, work with them to discover their unique strengths, and help eliminate the damage caused by their weaknesses. Coaching is not about duplicating the coach's exact approach or style. It is about helping clients realize unique skills and talents and to learn how to leverage their strengths to master the key fundamentals of success.

5. **Effective advising** – A coach must be able to listen fully to the client's challenges and issues and help the client respond effectively to specific problems or opportunities. The coach must be able to competently offer feedback, knowledge, and advice. Many people may be masters in their field but lack the ability to convey that knowledge to others.

Wright

Interesting; so how does the coaching process work?

Landram

The coaching process follows four guidelines:

1. **Set pre-determined goals and objectives** – Before actual work begins the coach and the client must agree on goals and objectives. For example, if you hired a fitness coach he or she must know if you want to improve cardiovascular fitness, increase your strength, or lose body fat. Each of these goals requires a very different fitness application.

2. **Use specific models** – The coach must employ very specific models to teach clients how to achieve their goals and objec-

tives. For example when I work with sales teams, I employ a client development system model. Not only must the clients decide where they want to go (their goals and objectives), but the coach must provide a model (a vehicle) to reach those goals and objectives. Last year I began working with a sales team instructed to approach every prospect in their territory. Each salesperson had an average of 700 prospects. As a result, they were very busy but they were not successfully converting prospects into customers. We launched a client development system model that helped them identify more ideal key targets and construct appropriate approaches. The team's production increased fifty percent within three months.

3. **Utilize a behavioral assessment** – Coaches should utilize a behavioral assessment, such as the DiSC® Personal Profile System. An assessment tool of this type helps the coach understand how his or her client prefers to communicate and the client's preferred learning style. With this knowledge the coach can then adapt his or her communication style to that of the client.

4. **Coach on the telephone** – Many coaching professionals believe that coaching must be conducted face-to-face. According to the research of Dr. Albert Mehrabian, when people are communicating face-to-face and speaking the same language, seven percent of meaning is expressed through words, thirty-eight percent through verbals (pitch, speed, volume, tone), and fifty-five percent through non-verbals (facial expressions, posture, gestures). In my years of experience I have coached in both environments. I have found that a telephone appointment allows the client and the coach to dig more deeply and comfortably into subjects by eliminating one of the channels of communication. Over the telephone, seven percent of meaning is conveyed by words and a full ninety-three percent of meaning is communicated through verbals. Neither the client nor the coach become distracted or affected by the non-verbals.

Wright

Would you describe for our readers some important areas of exploration that help maximize the client relationship?

Landram

Focusing on four key areas maximizes the investment in the coaching relationship. They are the critical success factors of the client's profession, interpersonal skills, mental strength and stamina, and accountability.

David, let's explore each of these areas more fully because they are so important:

1. **Critical success factors** – Each profession has a list of critical success factors or fundamentals that one must master. Some of the critical success factors of a master salesperson are prospecting, scheduling appointments, and overcoming objections. A coach helps clients identify their critical success factors and then creates a customized plan to enable salespeople to master them.

2. **Interpersonal skills** – No one succeeds alone. To reach high levels of success we must employ the help, advice, and guidance of others. This requires that we develop special communication skills. Often the content in a coaching session is centered on teaching the client skills to effectively coach, guide, persuade, reprimand, or strengthen relationships key to the client's success. The coach can help guide the client successfully through a web of highly interdependent relationships.

3. **Mental strength and stamina** – Many people say that success requires ten percent skill and ninety percent attitude. This is mostly true. Often, however, people searching to improve their attitude are searching for the wrong cure. People are often on a quest to "permanently fix" or "perfect their attitude." Unfortunately, what is misunderstood is that there isn't a cure to maintain a permanent, positive attitude. We must work on it daily. A friend once gave me an illustration that helped me understand this fully. Mark Willis, President of Keller Williams Realty, said, "Staying motivated is like taking a shower. Just because you bathed today doesn't mean you will be clean tomorrow. You must bathe regularly to stay clean." The coach should provide the client with enhanced skills and tools to maintain motivation and a positive mental attitude over time.

4. **Accountability** – Every one of us will perform better when we believe someone is watching us or cares about our success.

Both working hard and committing to success are easy when we feel good. Accountability helps us to stay focused and to keep working on the days when we don't "feel like it." I know if I had a totally open schedule that allowed me to go to the gym any time of the day, exercise would be easy. However, I can't. I must awaken at 4:30 A.M. and be at the gym at 5:00 A.M. I never "feel like" exercising at that time of day. My personal fitness coach provides me with the accountability I need to get positive results. Coaching helps clients maintain their consistency. All achievement is obtained by consistently applying fundamentals over time.

Wright

According to your research, you maintain an individual's results will be four times greater when coaching is combined with training. Why is that so?

Landram

We know in teaching children that we must give them repeated exposure and practice to master a concept. Remember, David, when we were learning to print the letters of the alphabet? Our teachers didn't show us the letters once and expect us to know them. No, we spent months learning one letter at a time with a myriad of applications. Somehow we often forget this as adult learners. We often believe that if we want to learn something we can take a one-day seminar or read one book on the subject. Of course, a one-time event does not lead to mastery. Anything we do well, whether it is golf, sailing, or even making a bed, requires repeated attempts and practice. In working with my clients, I recognize that they receive a much higher return on their investment if they are provided with an opportunity for group learning and given time for one-on-one coaching to review and successfully implement the skills focused on in the group setting.

Wright

So if I were going to search out a coach, how long would it take for me to fix my issues or how long should a person engage in the coaching process?

Landram

This is a very interesting area of exploration, David. When someone asks me this question, I respond that they should be coached forever. People are often shocked. One of the most important principles of maintaining success and mastery is to understand there is no "quick fix" or "quick route." Lasting success and mastery come by identifying, perfecting, and repeatedly implementing a very few key fundamentals. Most people become bored with fundamentals. The right coach helps you stay focused on the "boring stuff." As long as the coaching relationship is positive and you are growing and succeeding, you should continue. If not, change coaches but don't stop the coaching process.

Wright

So how does an individual learn to reinforce the skills learned during the coaching relationship?

Landram

Let me give you an illustration. I coach a salesperson who would consistently become very upset when he opened his daily sales production report. If the numbers were lower than he expected he would fret about being behind. If the numbers were high, he would fret that he wouldn't be able to maintain the pace. It became distracting and started negatively impacting his productivity.

Through repeated discussion during subsequent coaching sessions I taught him to focus on the activities that lead to his desired results. I had him focus on prospecting, and setting and conducting appointments instead of focusing on the numbers on the reports. With repeated conditioning he understands that focusing on the right activities will lead to the right results.

Today when he opens his sales production report he accepts the numbers. If they are too low, he sets more appointments with people who meet his ideal client profile. If the numbers are on target, he continues to prospect and set appointments.

Wright

I've always thought that with your attorney, or with a coach, or someone who is was trying to help, you need to be completely honest about everything. You need to be open about your business and about what you're trying to accomplish. That's kind of risky for me. How much importance do you place on privacy with the people you're coaching?

Landram

Transparency in the coaching relationship is paramount. For a coach to truly help a client, there must be an open relationship. As a result, the client is vulnerable. If the coach passes judgment and is not discreet the relationship is destroyed. One has to be very careful when selecting an individual to enter his or her life at this level. This topic must be discussed at the very beginning and the two individuals must outline specific guidelines and expectations of the relationship.

Wright

I have one more question about this subject. How would I go about finding out if a coach is really good?

Landram

The easiest way to find a very good coach is by referral. However, if you aren't able to locate someone by referral, then find an individual who exhibits the four characteristics I mentioned earlier. Great coaches are willing to give an individual time to explore areas of focus with you. After discussing some of your issues and challenges you will be able to ascertain whether or not that coach is competent and whether or not there is a good fit.

Wright

One thing I've known through the years is that to call someone "coach" is to speak of them with high praise. I remember back in junior high school (which would be fifty-five years or so ago) there was a man there who was the "coach" and all the boys and the girls loved him universally. Years later, before he died, I saw him at a football game. I looked at him and called him coach and it seemed to please him.

Landram

Yes, coaching is a very honorable profession. Coaching involves taking clients' lives in your care. You can't do that lightly. You must treat the relationship with great respect. I personally can't believe I get to do this every day. It is absolutely incredible. It is my mission to help spare my clients from the struggles, defeat, and pain I experienced in my long crawl to success. Hopefully they realize success on a path of lesser resistance by leveraging my pain and the lessons I've learned. When I am working with an individual and they call me to share a success based on the lessons we've discussed and worked on together, it's an incredible reward.

Wright

Well, what an interesting conversation and what an interesting and necessary occupation you have. I really appreciate all this time you've taken with me to answer these questions.

Landram

Well, David, thank you so very much for letting me be part of this project. Most people want to succeed. You are helping people identify the keys to getting there.

Wright

Today we've been talking with Charlotte Palmer Landram. She uniquely combines coaching with training and development programs for companies all over the United States, Canada, Australia, and the United Kingdom. I think we've found out today that she really knows what she's talking about.

Thank you so much for being with us, Charlotte, on *Masters of Success*.

Landram

It's been a genuine pleasure discussing these vital issues with you.

About The Author

Charlotte Palmer Landram creates and leads customized training and development programs. She conducts workshops across the United States and Canada as well as in Australia and the United Kingdom. Her highly effective approach is to combine group education with a series of follow-up coaching sessions with individual participants. *"The results achieved are four times greater when excellent training is combined with professional coaching,"* says Charlotte.

For eight years Charlotte was one of First American Title Insurance Company's most effective title sales representatives. Working in Houston, Texas she was the featured sales coach on a weekly radio program. She was also a regular columnist in *Real Estate and You*, a journal reaching over 17,000 Realtors. Charlotte's articles on business development, improving sales skills, and enhancing customer service appear in numerous real estate and business journals and in such national sales magazines as *Selling Power*.

Charlotte's industry experience also includes leading one of Keller Williams Realty's top market centers of 210 real estate agents that generated more than 460 million dollars in sales revenue in 2003. She attributes the success of the company to the use of a systematic approach to business development that combined a vigorous schedule of workshops with one-on-one coaching. Charlotte is a skilled workshop facilitator and a dedicated, supportive sales and leadership coach who helps her clients achieve their professional and business goals.

Charlotte Palmer Landram

High Impact Training & Coaching Systems

Phoenix, Arizona

Email: charlotte@highimpactsystems.com

www.highimpactsystems.com

Chapter Sixteen

JOHN CHRISTENSEN

THE INTERVIEW

David Wright (Wright)
Today we are talking with John Christensen. John's story begins in the shipping department at ChartHouse Learning where he began working as a teenager for his father, Ray. He worked his way to the top the old fashioned way—having to prove to his father and the company that he was a real filmmaker who could tell moving stories.

Today Mr. Christensen guides ChartHouse as "playground director"—business talk for CEO—with an inspiring vision of an engaged workplace that can be developed through the "Fish! Philosophy®." ChartHouse Learning is changing the way business is done worldwide. As his dad before him, John created an eloquent language to transform lives. In 1997, he translated what happens daily at Seattle's world famous Pike Place Fish Market's culture into a vital global learning program called Fish! and changed the entire business film industry. In the process, John also achieved his lifelong dream to turn workplaces into energetic, creative, and wholehearted endeavors with the four simple principles embodied in the Fish! Philosophy.

John Christensen, welcome to *The Masters of Success*.

John Christensen (Christensen)

Thank you, David. I appreciate that.

Wright

John, obviously, my first question is what are the four simple principles of the Fish! Philosophy?

Christensen

The four simple principles are "play," "make their day," "be there," and "choose your attitude."

Wright

Play? In other words we're supposed to play at work?

Christensen

Yes. Play is the basis of where creativity and innovation happens. If you look back into your own life and see where you were most creative, it was during those moments of play and inspiration, where you got lost in the moment. We call that "play." Now, if that scares corporations, think of it as "lightheartedness." Think of it as taking your work seriously, but taking yourself lightheartedly.

Wright

So tell us a little bit about what you do at ChartHouse Learning.

Christensen

We are kind of like cultural anthropologists. We study things that are out in the world, and then we help put a language to it. For instance, that's what I saw at the fish market. I saw these fishmongers being totally engaged in their work and I thought, "Wait a minute! Wait a minute! There's something deeper going on than just play and all this craziness I see on the shop floor." So we interpreted that, then put a language around it, and helped get it out into the business world; not only the business world, however, schools are using it, too.

Wright

When you say "language," you're talking about terms that can be understood universally?

Christensen

Yes, absolutely. In Fish! it's ancient wisdom that's been resurfaced and presented in a new way and in an unlikely place—a fish market.

Wright

While preparing for this interview, I read that the first film in your series titled, *The Business of Paradigms*™, is the best selling business film of all time. Is that true?

Christensen

Yes.

Wright

My goodness!

Christensen

Yes. That film was first created in the '80s by my father and futurist Joel Barker. It's been translated into many, many languages. *Fish!* is creeping up there, though. It's going to surpass *The Business of Paradigms*™ someday.

Wright

When you speak and train, how do you motivate people to create workplaces that are joyful and innovative, lighthearted, and wholehearted?

Christensen

The interesting part of all this is when we tell them about it and they see the film or read the book, there's something that connects inside them that says either they had this in them or they were searching for this—this lightheartedness—this engagement of being at work and being engaged in what you do. We've made a film series with a poet named David White. David talks about being wholehearted. He has a friend—a monk—who said, "The way around burnout isn't necessarily burnout. It's being wholehearted in what you do." Now that's incredible. What it means is, if you come to work and you're totally engaged and enjoy what you are doing, the day goes by much quicker and you're going to be connected to it.

Wright

Do you find many CEOs, or especially upper management people, who are a little—

Christensen

Apprehensive of this?

Wright

Yes.

Christensen

Yes, there are. But for the corporations that embrace it and "get it," stand back—watch out for their organizations! For instance, the CEO of Aspen Ski Co., a ski company in Aspen, Colorado, who has embraced it said, "This is the pull; this is what we're going to be. This is the way we're going to service our employees. We're going to be engaged with what we do." They have 3500 seasonal employees. They teach them every year. They teach them the Fish! Philosophy when the new group comes in, or even when part of the old group comes back in. They resurface the philosophy and say, "Remember—be engaged." When they open that playing field and give them the boundaries of saying, "Okay, safety is first in any business; here are the playing fields. Be safe. Don't do anything that's rude or crude," they saw things happening.

For example, a guy—a young man—created his own super hero called "Captain Iowa." He'd fly kids through the lift line up to the front and he'd help create an atmosphere that was "engaging" in the lift line. It distracted people when they were standing there for twenty-five minutes waiting for their turn on the ski lift. They also started karaoke in the waiting lines and they do limbo. Now, that created an atmosphere because, again, the CEO is saying, "Look, we have great snow and the same mountains as the other resorts. What separates us from our other ski resort business friends?" The difference was the way they engaged with customers. That's the way, first and foremost, to have people engage in their work and be happy with where they are. I'm not just talking about a "Pollyannaish" kind of happy, happy workplace, I'm talking about people being engaged in what they do. Now, if you have that and you create that kind of atmosphere, watch out! Your bottom line is going to go up and your employee turnover is going to go down.

Another thing we find that's just really amazing is, when you step back and analyze it, we're in our places of work more than we are in our places of worship, more than we are in the great outdoors, and more than we are with our families. Now, if we can't connect to that, be engaged, and take joy in what we're doing, that's a sad commentary on our life. What are you giving up your hours for? What are you spending your life's energy on? What are you giving, where are you investing your energy—your life energy? Is this the place you really want to be? Is this the place that's going to make you flourish?

Wright

What do you mean by "make their day?" Are these management theories that apply to employees, or are these employee theories that apply to customers?

Christensen

It applies absolutely to everyone. It's employee-to-employee, it's employer-to-employee, and it's employee-to-customer. It's the whole thing. What I'm saying is coming to work with that attitude realizing your life is about what are you are giving to people. "Make their day" is just a new way of saying it—make people's day.

Serving others is when we really find joy. It doesn't matter if the CEO is talking to a vice-president or to a president, or if an employee is talking to a guest in a hotel, the philosophy is, make people's day! And it doesn't take much; the stories we hear about the little nuances of what makes people's day are amazing. I mean, just being with a person moves us into "being there." What does "being there" mean? It means just being in the moment with a person. For example, if you're trying to talk to somebody in your office while you've got the phone ringing, and you've got a message coming in on your cell phone, put it all away. Let voicemail answer the phone, put the cell phone away, and really be there with the person. When you're really in the presence of a person, they can feel it.

Do I have time to share a story with you?

Wright

Sure.

Christensen

There was a prison guard who was in the service area of a jail; he was the "booking agent" shall we say. The police department he worked for went through the Fish! Philosophy teaching and he became aware of being present and making people's day. The prison guard was totally in the moment with someone who was being booked for shoplifting. He gave the person dignity and respect. The prisoner started to weep, saying, "I've never been treated this way in my life, much less while I'm being booked for a crime I know I did." That's being present. The prison guard made that guy's day! It might have made a huge difference in that guy's life too maybe—who knows?

Fish! brings to the surface what people have in them. It gives them a way to say, "I can do this—I have permission. My organization has shown me the light of being "a day-maker."

Be private with people. When you're choosing your attitude, making people's day, and being present for people, guess what? The appropriate "play" comes out.

Wright

In reference to the third principle—"choose your attitude"—we're publishing a book for a man now about attitude. One of his favorite sayings is, "The difference between a good day and a bad day is your attitude."

Christensen

Absolutely. We all have magnificent stories about our lives. But if you look at people who have tragedies in some respect, and they come in to work whistling, what is that? How would we face some of these tragedies if they happen to us? That is what we mean by "choose your attitude."

Wright

John, I'd like to quote something you said referring to business. The quote is, "We need people who are passionate, committed, and free to live the organization's vision through their personal value." Could you explain what you were talking about?

Christensen

Yes. When you have an alignment with what you stand for as an individual and what the company—the organization—is standing for, step out of the way—watch out! Watch the power that happens to that.

Wright

When you talk about businesses, you use words like "love" and "soul."

Christensen

Right.

Wright

Most people would think that spiritual values would not be appropriate in a business setting. Do companies accept your spiritual values as necessary ingredients to success?

Christensen

There's a whole new movement out there about spirituality. I want it to be clear—we're not talking religion. We're talking about the spirit and soul of people and these elements bring the soul of a business alive.

We made a film with Southwest Airlines. Herb Kelleher and Rollin King founded Southwest Airlines stating, "We wanted to create a workplace based on love rather than fear." Now, if Southwest Airlines with 33,000 employees is based on love and is doing incredibly well in the airline industry, is that not a valuable statement to everybody in business?

Wright

Is there anything or anyone in your life who has made a difference for you and helped you to become a better person?

Christensen

I have a lot of mentors in my life. My parents have been incredible mentors. My mom was a social worker and a very incredible people-oriented woman; my dad was an artist. Combined, they have been wonderful mentors for me. I've also had the blessing of having Ken Blanchard as a mentor and Spencer Johnson, so I've had great mentors in that respect, too.

Wright

I was talking to Jim Cathcart the other day. I told him that one of my mentors had no knowledge of his being a mentor—Bill Gove from Florida. I have been listening to his talks and tapes and reading his books for probably forty years.

What do you think makes up a mentor? In other words, are there characteristics that mentors seem to have in common?

Christensen

I believe they're different for everybody. I mean, everyone finds a different mentor. I think some of the most beautiful mentorships happen when a person takes you under his or her wing.

Another inspiration for me is Norman Vincent Peale. Okay, he's got religion in there, but his books and writings were a type of mentorship for me. His presence, the way he spoke so eloquently and had so much passion mentored me.

Many different things can inspire you. If a tape or a book inspires you and that tool becomes your mentor—fabulous. When it opens you up to the possibilities in your life, whether it is a book, a personal relationship, a tape, a film, these are all wonderful aspects of opening you up to possibilities.

Wright

I remember when I was in Seattle a few years ago and saw the people working in the fish company you wrote about, I remember two feelings about them: One was a feeling that this would be a nice place to buy something; but the biggest feeling was these guys are really happy and are having fun. And they've got a tough job too—it's not the kind of job a bank president would have.

Christensen

No. Hey, they don't work in air conditioning and heating. They work with dead fish, ice, and on cold cement floors. I've wiped out there many a time. It's just showing you the possibilities when workers like them can practice those principles successfully with their hands in dead fish, cold ice, during twelve-hour days. That's what's so powerful about it. That's why we call it the Fish! Philosophy. It's based on the fact that if the fish market workers can do it, you can do it. The philosophy comes from ancient wisdom and was noticed as a practice among sellers in that fish market. If folks in a fish market can do it, we can all do it.

Wright

We've talked about three out of four of the principles. The last one I'd like to ask you about is the principle "be there." Do you mean come to work on time and be there? Or be there for people?

Christensen

Be there for people. I mean absolutely be in the moment. As I was saying, when you're with somebody, put the other things down. I catch myself so many times sitting at my desk when people come in, and I'm reading something at the time. I'm just half with them. You have to take that moment and put down what you're doing and be there for them.

Another good little exercise to do is when the phone rings, take a moment before you pick it up and just pause. Think about what you're going to do on the phone. It doesn't matter if it's a sales person or whomever; just remember to be there in the moment when you're on the phone with a person. It's an interesting little exercise of being present.

Wright

Most people are fascinated with these new television programs about being a survivor. What has been the greatest comeback you have made from adversity in your career or in your life?

Christensen

Wow! The biggest adversity? Well, there are two. We went through a stint with a company where some people tried to take over our business, and I made it through that. But one of the things was living up to my mentor's—my father's—image and knowing in my heart and in my gut that I had the capacity to lead the company and to be a great filmmaker like my father. And I don't mean great in a cocky way—I'm saying bringing what we bring to the table regarding documentaries; showing the world what the possibilities are. That's what I mean by "great." That was a high; but it was a hurdle to work through also.

Wright

When I was researching for this interview, I noticed on your Web site Joel Barker, the futurist who helped your father, was also referred to.

Christensen

Futurist, correct.

Wright

And so your father started making what, documentary films?

Christensen

Yes. He started off in advertising just when television was getting started in the late '50s. He happened to be in love with the documentary approach. He pursued the documentarian lifestyle and would go off and make films. What he brought to the table was this uniqueness—this anthropological aspect of looking at something, studying it, and saying what can we do to show that?

For instance, when his career started off in Omaha, Nebraska, he made a film about the city of Omaha. But through the whole film, you didn't know where you were until the end of the film, *Come See Our City, Omaha*. But it showed you who the people were, what the organizations were like in Omaha, and it persuaded you that you'd like to come and live there and build your business there. So he brought that approach to it (i.e., let's study it, let's bring it; let's show people what it's about instead of telling them).

Again, that's what happened with the paradigm idea. Let's look at a paradigm; let's look at it all these different ways. If it doesn't get you this way, look at it that way. If this story doesn't connect with you, look at it another way, then perhaps you can relate to *that* way.

Wright

The freewheeling workplace of the 1990s is long gone. Companies are cutting perks. Employees are reverting from casual attire to business wear. How can employees really "play" at work when the reins are being pulled back so tightly?

Christensen

Well, that's our point—the reigns shouldn't be pulled back so tightly. Ken Blanchard calls it the "tight underwear syndrome." We need to get rid of that. We need to free people up because when you're free is when creativity and innovation happens. I don't know where the quote comes from, but it was said, "If 'work' was 'play,' Silicon Valley would not have been created." Two guys in their garage—Bill Hewlett and Dave Packard—I mean how many guys were playing— tinkering around, right? And they came up with the Hewlett-Packard audio oscillator and went on to make computers, printers, etc. And with Apple computers, the Apple I was Steven Wozniak's first contribution to the personal computer field. I mean how many more can we list? These folks were playing and came up with some of the most innovative ideas in their field!

Back to the original idea, it's the playfulness—how we saw the fishmongers reacting to each other and reacting to customers at the fish market. You can see what they're doing and make your own style based on that. It opens you up to saying, "What can *we* do that's about playfulness?"

Wright

I've heard about the impact Fish! is having on corporate America. Has it been used outside the business world?

Christensen

Schools are among our biggest clientele. It's amazing! We're now creating a curriculum for schools and we're working on creating how to interpret this and bring it into the classroom. If you could talk about, "play," "being present," "choose your attitude," and "make people's day" with elementary students, imagine what possibilities lie in the future for that.

Wright

Are you having more success getting it into the private schools or public schools?

Christensen

Public schools are embracing it. First and foremost right now, what's happening is that administrators and teachers are being brought into discussions about how we can engage them with our work. It goes back to discovering what kind of organization we can be and how we're going to help people be engaged in what we're here for, whether the business is a hospital, a school, or a manufacturing plant.

We worked with a roofing company that used this philosophy and it turned their entire company around. Now they're a world famous roofing company; they get roofing jobs in different places throughout the world. How did they do this? They changed their philosophy and became more effective in how they do business.

Now back to education and using this philosophy in the classroom. If you are a teacher being present in the classroom for your kids— they're the customers—you have to serve them. How about your partner? They're there to teach you as much as you are there to teach them. My goodness! I mean that was my first love—I wanted to be a teacher asking, "What can you bring to the table?" The kind of teacher we need is like the English professor John Keating in the movie *Dead Poets Society*. We need teachers who are engaged with the minds of our youth asking how do I get to them? How do I reach them? How can I be there with them? What do I do to make their day?

We're actually working on the concept of saying that the four principles of Fish! are the rules of the classroom by asking the questions such as, "What am I doing today to play—to be playful?" This works both ways. This is teacher-to-student and partner-to-partner philosophy. What are we doing to make the classroom fun? What are we doing to make each other's day? How am I being there for you? How are you being there for me? How are you being there for your peers? And first and foremost, how are you choosing to come to school? How are you choosing to "be here" today—what is your attitude?

Wright

Very interesting. Boy, this has been a fast, fast thirty minutes, and I really do appreciate your being a guest today on *The Masters of Success*. I really appreciate your taking the time.

Christensen

Well, David, thank you, and thanks for helping spread the word.

Wright

Today we have been talking with John Christensen whose story began, as he said, working with his father who is a great role model for him. And you've heard how the Fish! Philosophy can literally change you and your company's future, as it's changing the future for many companies in America. I'd like to shamelessly advertise the book; I think everyone should read it. I know you're making good at Amazon.com. Can people get it directly from you or can they find out more on your Web site? If you'll give us that information, I would appreciate it.

Christensen

Absolutely, it is ChartHouse.com. On the site you can go to fish-philosophy.com, which is an entire Web site with all the Fish! information. You can purchase our films as well as our ancillary products, our fishing gear, and you can purchase the books. Now there are two books on the market, David. There's *First Fish!* and our second book that came out called *Fish Tales*.

Wright

Well, I hope our readers will rush to the Web site and get this book. I've got *Fish Tales*, now I'm going to get the first one.

Christensen

Thank you, David. Thank you so much. I really appreciate your time.

About The Author

John Christensen's story begins in the shipping department at ChartHouse Learning where he began working as a teenager for his father, Ray. He worked his way to the top the old-fashioned way, proving to his father—and the company—that he was a real filmmaker who could tell moving stories. Today Christensen guides ChartHouse as "Playground Director" (CEO in business-speak) with an inspiring vision of an engaged workplace that can be developed through the FISH! Philosophy. The rest of the story is that ChartHouse Learning is changing the way business is done worldwide.

Like his dad before him, John's created an eloquent language to transform lives. In 1998, he translated what happens daily at Seattle's world famous Pike Place Fish Market's culture into a viable global learning program called FISH! and changed the entire business film industry. In the process, John also achieved his lifelong dream of how to turn workplaces into energetic, creative and wholehearted endeavors with the four simple principles embodied in the FISH! Philosophy: • PLAY• MAKE THEIR DAY• BE THERE• CHOOSE YOUR ATTITUDE.

Today John speaks to vastly different organizations about his journey—the serendipitous discovery of the fish market—and how that simple FISH! Philosophy he and his team poetically articulated on film four years ago can dramatically change the stories of companies and individuals.

John Christensen

www.charthouse.com

www.fishphilopophy.com

Chapter Seventeen

MIKE VAN HOOZER

David Wright (Wright)

Today we're talking with Mike Van Hoozer. Mike Van Hoozer is a gifted communicator and coach, an insightful author and consultant, and a devoted husband and father of five boys. Mike has dedicated his life to making an impact in the lives of other people. For over seventeen years, he has worked with every kind of organization including small startup companies, Fortune 50 companies, professional athletes, churches, and non-profit organizations. In his work with clients, Mike focuses on helping individuals and organizations reach their maximum potential through workshops, retreats, coaching, and consulting. Mike is a member of the National Speakers Association and is sought out as a speaker for organizations and businesses on the topics of leadership, teamwork, passion, purpose, significance, and work/life balance.

Mike is Founder and President of Van Hoozer and Associates, a leadership think tank, and also works with the Total BEST Group helping individuals and organizations pursue the disciplines of Balance, Excellence, Service, and Truth.

Mike, welcome to *Masters of Success*.

Mike Van Hoozer (Van Hoozer)
Thank you David, it's a pleasure to be here.

Wright
Mike, you speak on a lot of topics but one of the topics you're most passionate about is leadership. Why are you so passionate about teaching and developing leaders?

Van Hoozer
It's the biggest thank-you I could give to the many mentors and leaders I've had in my life, going back to my grandfather, basketball coaches, and leaders I've had in my professional life. I'm very passionate about passing on the same qualities and characteristics of leadership to future generations of leaders as well. We have such a bright, energetic, and innovative talent pool that's coming out to the work force, I want to do everything I can to help those leaders and perpetuate what I think is a character-based leadership legacy.

Wright
So what characteristics or qualities do you think make a good leader?

Van Hoozer
The following pairs of words describe the essence of leadership:

Vision and Vulnerability—Vision is seeing things not as they are but as they should be and breathing hope into the dreams and aspirations of the people who follow you. On the vulnerability side, that's a characteristic we don't often associate with leadership; but I think leaders need to be more vulnerable in saying things like, "I don't know," or, "What do you think about that?"

Jim Collins recently wrote about how great decisions are made in companies. In his research, he discovered great decisions begin with an honest and sincere approach to being vulnerable and saying things like, "I don't know."

Passion and Perseverance—Passion is something that ignites the will to achieve that which the mind has conceived. Perseverance is overcoming obstacles and achieving the impossible.

Competence and Caring—People want leaders who are competent and who know what they're talking about. They also want leaders who care about their people's potential to be. Caring is not a word we often associate in the business world; but I think caring is a word that definitely will contribute to the success of people in excellent and effective organizations.

Wright

You're the father of five boys—the coach of your own Van Hoozer basketball team—have you learned any lessons from being the father of five boys?

Van Hoozer

I sure have. The first thing is I have an awesome and wonderful wife who helps me in developing these boys. Individually I think, from having five boys I've learned how important it is to develop their individual gifts and talents. When I come home I spend time with them as a group, but I also spend time with each of my boys individually. I try to invest time nurturing them in what they're interested in and passionate about, not what I'm interested in or necessarily what the other boys are interested in. If I'm spending one-on-one time with one of my sons I want to make sure that I nurture him to be the best he can be.

I also think quality time fits within the context of quantity of time. Some people can mistakenly say (and I've heard people give me this advice) it's not the quantity of time—it's the quality of the time. It's actually *both*. We can't expect to have a scheduled thirty minutes of quality time. That time fits within the context of the quantity of time spent.

My parents were divorced when I was three, and I didn't have a father growing up. I've come to the conclusion that it's unique that we have five boys. A good friend once told me, "There's a reason you have all boys, especially since you grew up without a father. Your mission in life is to raise a legacy of fathers." I'm very passionate about this mission. At the end of my life, I'm not going to wish I had spent more time at work.

Wright

You're also a personal coach and work with a wide variety of clients including business professionals and professional athletes. In working with your coaching clients, what is your goal?

Van Hoozer

My ultimate goal is to help them reach their maximum potential and help them discover their calling and purpose—that's what we work on. I want people to focus on what they feel they were called to do and why they were put on this earth.

Wright

So how do you do this?

Van Hoozer

I love the quote by Benjamin Zander who's the conductor of the Boston Philharmonic Orchestra. He wrote a great book called *The Art of Possibility*. In that book he said, "I make myself a relentless architect of the possibilities of human beings." I always look for that and it is something I use in my coaching, my leadership, and my speaking as well—to make myself a relentless architect of the possibilities of human beings, constantly talk about their potential to be, and help them to reach their maximum potential. Whether I'm giving positive encouragement and feedback, or constructive feedback, I want them to know I'm on their side. I'm doing that in the context of talking about them becoming the person they desire and were meant to be.

Wright

You recently wrote a new book, *Applied Leadership: Putting Theory into Pra*ctice. In that book you wrote that people development was "the hard side of business." Tell me what you mean by that.

Van Hoozer

When I would deliver leadership workshops, I was always struck by the fact that people would think people development was "soft"— the fluffy stuff that had no place in business. The hard stuff was numbers, making the numbers, and focusing on those types of things. What I've discovered is that the hard (meaning "difficult") part of leadership—the thing that nobody wants to sign up for—is developing people. In business school, you learn about making the numbers, accounting, economics, finance, and other things you need to know in business. People rarely attend leadership training to learn how to give feedback, how to coach people, and how to lead people. I think these are the really "difficult" aspects of leadership, and people development is directly related to the bottom line.

Wright

How do you define success?

Van Hoozer

For me, success is living a life of excellence, using the gifts and talents I've been given to their fullest, and focusing on making an impact in the lives of other people. That is very important to me and that's my personal mission statement or purpose as well. I want to continue to focus on making an impact on the lives of other people and using the gifts and talents I've been given to be able to do that. At the end of the day, if I've made an impact on people in my speaking and my coaching in organizations, and in my personal life with my boys and my wife, I consider that success.

Wright

Another topic you speak about is finding purpose and passion in work and life. How do people discover their purpose?

Van Hoozer

Turn off their cell phones! Joking aside, I think it's cutting out the noise and chaos and clutter of this life. Once we do that, we need to take time to reflect on questions such as: Why are we here and what is our reason for being? We know those are important questions, but we rarely spend time on them. Many times, we think more about **time** than **direction**. We focus on activities such as getting to the next client meeting, and other things we have to go and do, but we don't invest time pondering the more directional questions. Our purpose in life is the most important thing we have to consider—it determines our values, our direction in life, and why we're here. I think cutting out the noise, chaos, and clutter to spend time to reflect on purpose and direction is one of the most important and worthwhile investments of our time.

Wright

So what do you see is your purpose in life?

Van Hoozer

My purpose, as I see it, is living for what matters most and making my life count. In addition, I strive to shine the spotlight on the Star of the story of life—not on me. I think we often try to craft our own stories and if we were screenwriters we would write our own script. There are certain people we would write into our script and there are certain people we would write out of our script; but we don't get that option. We are only here for a brief moment and our stories are just little stories.

For me, my faith is very important to me. I believe my life works best when I shine the spotlight on the real Star of the story of life—God.

Wright

Who are some of the role models in your life?

Van Hoozer

My mom had a big impact on my life. She inspired confidence, gave me courage, and demonstrated perseverance as far as dealing with the life situations we had.

My grandfather, Pat Joyner, was very important to me as well. He defined integrity—what it was to be a man of integrity. He also showed me the value of mutual respect for people and taught me the Golden Rule—doing to others as you would have them do to you.

My basketball coach, Walt Homan, was also very influential in my life. He taught me the same things—integrity and mutual respect as well as hard work and self-discipline.

Other people include my father-in-law, Barry Landrum, and my friend Louie Giglio. My father-in-law is a pastor and a great communicator. Louie is a speaker to thousands of college students and a great communicator. They have shown me what my real source of strength and power is and where that comes from.

Another mentor is Terrence Gee who has been a big influence on my life professionally, especially when I first started out as this energetic college student who was coming out to make a difference in the world. He demonstrated for me what an "invisible leader" looks like. He showed me the characteristics of leadership and modeled the way of effective leadership.

Wright

You deliver an entire workshop titled, "The Invisible Hand of Leadership." Did you get the idea from Terrence Gee? Are you really encouraging leaders to be "invisible"?

Van Hoozer

Yes, I got the idea from watching him. Ultimately, the title of the workshop is a play on words. The goal of the workshop is to create a generation of leaders who can survive and thrive when the teacher/mentor is no longer around. There's a lot of talk around succession planning and developing leaders within organizations now. Companies are starting to realize they need to do that.

What I discovered by observing Terrence and other leaders was that leaders should be both visible in somebody's life as well as invisible doing things behind the scenes. Sometimes things would happen and I would see that Terrence had been involved in it. I would recognize that it had his fingerprints all over it. He would also do things behind the scenes that he would not take credit for. We need to encourage leaders to do more of this selfless leadership versus self-serving leadership. After leaders become visible, active, and make an impact in the lives of their future leaders, they need to give these new leaders a chance to lead and affect new generations of leaders.

This concept is like a generation of families with my boys. I not only consider my children but also my children's children and their children—people I may never meet. I constantly ask myself: How can I develop my boys to lead and pass on those qualities and those values to future generations of leaders (their children)?

Wright

You also work with an organization called Total BEST delivering workshops on how to incorporate the disciplines of Balance, Excellence, Service, and Truth. A mantra of this workshop is, "By design, not default." How do we pursue a life by design and not by default?

Van Hoozer

We don't believe that everything's going to work out perfectly but having a plan and strategy definitely helps. What we teach in this workshop is that a lot of people are intentional in certain areas of their life. For instance, in work, sometimes we're very intentional about that. We have a strategy—a plan—and we have a career development map we're pursuing. In other areas, however, we let it happen by default, whether it is our spiritual life, or our finances, or our family. We may have those roles but we're letting things happen by default—we do not have a strategy for them.

What we encourage in this workshop is to truly pursue life by design—to be intentional in all areas of life, to have a strategy, to have a plan, and to unleash all of who you are in everything you do. I think that is critical to effective and successful living.

I have never had a client say, "Mike, I just want to pursue a life of mediocrity this year. I want that to be my annual theme. As my personal coach, I want you to help me with mediocrity in my life. In my physical fitness life, I want to be a couch potato, and I want you to hold me accountable—I want to write that down as a goal." No one truly desires mediocrity. By default, however, mediocrity sometimes seeps in because people are intentional in certain areas of their life and less in others.

That's what the mantra is really all about.

Wright

How do you want to be remembered?

Van Hoozer

That is one of the deep questions we ponder in our workshops and in a lot of the speaking I do. I try to get people to think about what they want their epitaph to be, and we talk about stories around that as well.

I mentioned that faith is very important to me. When I think about this question, I want to be remembered as a person who loved Jesus with all his heart and in turn, shared that love with his wife and five boys first, then the rest of his family, and then with others he came in contact with through speaking, coaching, and making an impact in the lives of people.

Wright

When you look back and consider all the decisions you've made in your lifetime having to do with both business and personal, has faith played an important role in that?

Van Hoozer

It definitely has, including getting in touch with purpose. I think so many people can spend time on the question of "why I am here." We look to faith to give us contentment and ultimately, for me and I think really for everybody, that this is where they're going to find true joy and contentment. If you find contentment there, then everything else is going to fall into place. Through our successes and trials, it gives us a foundation to stand on and it definitely has given me one. It can make everything more meaningful and more relevant in our lives as well.

What I've learned also professionally is that what I do is not necessarily what I'm called to do. What I mean by that is I feel that I've been gifted to pursue speaking, coaching, and the different avenues where I've worked in my career; but ultimately I have felt my life had a higher purpose.

My college roommate, James Stecker, helped me with this idea. James told me that we are all called to reach out and impact others regardless of our profession or path in life. Whether you are a pastor, professional athlete, college student, businessperson, mom, etc., your purpose revolves around the relationships in your life.

I look at some people whose identity is all tied up in their career or the place they worked for and it never transcends above that. When you look at what's happened in business during the last five years, some entire companies have gone out of business because of scandals or other kinds of misconduct. For people who worked there, their whole identity was tied up in that company and that's all there was for them. Then, when the organization and their job were both gone, they had nothing to fall back on to find a foundation in life, which is a tragedy. We are all on a quest for meaning and identity. Seeking the truth in my spiritual life has helped me discover my true identity.

Wright

What an interesting conversation, Mike. I really appreciate your taking all this time to answer these questions. I've learned a lot and I'm sure our readers will.

Van Hoozer

Thanks a lot for the opportunity to participate in this project.

Wright

Today we've been talking with Mike Van Hoozer. Mike is the founder and president of Van Hoozer and Associates, a leadership think tank. He also works with the Total BEST Group helping individuals and organizations pursue the disciplines of Balance, Excellence, Service, and Truth.

Mike, thank you so much for being with us today on *Masters of Success.*

About The Author

Mike Van Hoozer is a gifted communicator and coach, an insightful author, a consultant, and a devoted husband and father of five boys. He has dedicated his life to making an impact in the lives of other people. For over seventeen years, he has worked with every kind of organization including small startup companies, Fortune 50 companies, professional athletes, churches, and non-profit organizations. In his work with clients, Mike focuses on helping individuals and organizations reach their maximum potential through workshops, retreats, coaching, and consulting. Mike is a member of the National Speakers Association and is sought out as a speaker for organizations and businesses on the topics of leadership, teamwork, passion and purpose, significance, and work/life balance.

Mike is the Founder and President of Van Hoozer and Associates, a leadership think tank, and also works with the Total BEST Group helping individuals and organizations pursue the disciplines of Balance, Excellence, Service, and Truth.

Mike Van Hoozer

18219 TreeFork LN

Houston, TX 77094

Phone: 281.804.8041

Email: mvanhoozer@hotmail.com

Blog Site: www.vanhoozer.blogs.com

Web site: www.total-best.com